21st Century Knox

TITLES IN THE SERIES

21ST CENTURY FOUNDATIONS

Benjamin Armstrong, *editor*

In 1911 Capt. Alfred Thayer Mahan wrote in his book *Armaments and Arbitration,* "The study of military history lies at the foundation of all sound military conclusions and practices." One hundred years later, as we sail ever further into the twenty-first century, we are commonly told we face the most challenging circumstances in history, or that it is more dangerous now than ever before. These exaggerations tend to ignore the lessons of strategy and policy that come from our past.

The 21st Century Foundations series gives modern perspective to the great strategists and military philosophers of the past, placing their writings, principles, and theories within modern discussions and debates. Whether drawn from famous men or more obscure contributors with lesser known works, collecting and analyzing their writing will inform a new generation of students, military professionals, and policy makers alike. The essays and papers collected in this series are not provided in order to spell out cut and dry answers or exact procedures, but instead to help make sure we ask the right questions as we face the challenges of the future. The series informs the present by collecting and offering strategists and thinkers of the past.

21st Century Knox

Influence, Sea Power, and History for the Modern Era

EDITED BY DAVID KOHNEN

Naval Institute Press
Annapolis, Maryland

This book has been brought to publication with the generous assistance of Marguerite and Gerry Lenfest.

Naval Institute Press
291 Wood Road
Annapolis, MD 21402

Library of Congress Cataloging-in-Publication Data

Names: Knox, Dudley Wright, 1877–1960, author. | Kohnen, David, editor.
Title: 21st century Knox : influence, sea power, and history for the modern era / edited by David Kohnen.
Other titles: Twenty-first century Knox | Influence, sea power, and history for the modern era
Description: Annapolis, Maryland : Naval Institute Press, 2016. | Series: 21st century foundations | Includes bibliographical references.
Identifiers: LCCN 2015043438| ISBN 9781612519807 (alk. paper) | ISBN9781612519814 (mobi)
Subjects: LCSH: Knox, Dudley Wright, 1877–1960—Influence. | Naval art and science—United States—History—20th century—Sources. | Sea-power—United States—History—20th century—Sources. | United States. Navy—History. | United States—History, Naval.
Classification: LCC E748.K679 A3 2016 | DDC 359.00973—dc23
LC record available at http://lccn.loc.gov/2015043438

*To those who hold the line, stand the watch, and accept nothing more
than a sailor's ration . . .*

CONTENTS

ACKNOWLEDGMENTS

As a maritime historian, I greatly benefited from the encouragement and support of my mentors in my field. I am deeply indebted to Carl Boyd, Eminent Scholar Emeritus and Louis I. Jaffé Professor Emeritus of History, and the late Professor Craig M. Cameron of Old Dominion University. Through their encouragement, I ultimately completed additional graduate studies with John B. Hattendorf, the Ernest J. King Professor of Maritime History at the Naval War College. He assisted me in mining the rich cache of archival sources within the Naval Historical Collection of the Naval War College Archives and Library. During my doctoral studies at King's College London, I had the privilege of working under the immediate supervision of the Laughton Professor of Naval History in the Department of War Studies, Professor Andrew Lambert. Over the years, Lambert has encouraged me to continue examining the historiography of maritime literature, naval strategy, and intelligence.

As I retraced the naval and literary career of Knox, I received significant assistance from archivists and librarians. Papers relating to his work are scattered in various collections, including the National Archives and Records Administration, the Library of Congress, and the British National Archives. I offer my sincere thanks to the Naval Historical Foundation for assisting me in accessing records relating to Knox within their archives. I also wish to thank Rear Adm. Samuel Cox, USN (Ret.), and his staff at the Naval History and Heritage Command for facilitating my research in their expansive collections. I further extend special thanks to John Pentangelo and Evelyn Cherpack for their assistance in locating papers relating to Knox in the unique archival collections of the Naval War College. I am particularly indebted to the Knox family, especially his great-grandsons North and Peter Sturtevant, for their time in sharing their recollections and in reading early drafts of this book.

My colleagues at the Naval War College continuously challenged me to explain why history remains relevant as the U.S. Navy navigates future strategic questions of American sea power. In particular, I wish to thank all of my colleagues in the College of Operations and Strategic Leadership, the Naval War College Museum, and Naval War College Foundation. Professors Steven Kornatz, David Polatty, James Nordhill, Eric Dukat, and Lt. Col. Damian Spooner, USMC, in particular, helped me articulate why history remains relevant in ongoing efforts to anticipate the future influence of sea power upon the military policy of the United States. In this effort, I am especially grateful to Benjamin F. "B. J." Armstrong for his great assistance in preparing this manuscript for the Naval Institute Press's 21st Century Foundations series.

Historians often draw their freshest perspectives from their closest confidants. In this respect, I am most grateful for the ongoing encouragement of my wife, Dr. Sarah Goldberger, and our daughters, Elisabeth and Katherine. I am fortunate to have the unwavering support of Sarah, who holds a PhD in history. In all respects, this work was a collaborative effort, as she offered recommendations on early manuscript drafts. She also supported the expenditures and time required for my globetrotting as I pursued fresh archival leads during the course of my research. To Sarah, I extend my heartfelt thanks.

Below the Surface of Naval History

L eadership within the context of a given profession requires an informed understanding of a particular field of specialization. In maritime affairs, Commo. Dudley Wright Knox, USN, provided a singular example of leadership in his chosen profession. After graduating with the Naval Academy class of 1897, he proceeded to command a variety of war-ships in peacetime. He also served in combat operations during the 1898 Spanish-American War, the Boxer Rebellion, and the counterinsurgency in the Philippines, and he gained perspective on the higher levels of command as a staff officer during two world wars. Ultimately, conditioning in the American naval service inspired Knox to envision an American navy second to none. He developed a mature understanding of the nexus between peace and war. Crafting a distinctly maritime approach to address questions of strategy and policy in global affairs, Knox argued that navies provided the means "not to make war but to preserve peace, not to be predatory but to shield the free development of commerce, not to unsettle the world but to stabilize it through the promotion of law and order."[1]

Knox drew inspiration from ancestral connections with American history, which later informed his efforts to encourage fellow citizens to take an interest in their personal ties to the past. His father, Col. Thomas T. Knox, USA, gained fame fighting Native American tribes on the frontier, fought in the 1898 Spanish-American War, and helped frame American military strategy during the early twentieth century. Closely associated with Lt. Gen. Arthur MacArthur, Thomas T. Knox encouraged the marriage of his son, Dudley, to Lilly Hazard McCalla—daughter of Rear Adm. Bowman Hendry McCalla and sister of Mary McCalla, herself the wife of Lt. Arthur MacArthur II. Among other familial associations, Dudley maintained correspondence with Arthur's more famous brother, Douglas.

The Knox and MacArthur families loomed large in American history, which inspired Dudley throughout a career in the naval service of the United States. In his personal life, he encouraged his son, Cdr. Dudley Sargent Knox of the U.S. Navy Reserve, to take an interest in their heroic traditions, Brahmin heritage, and namesake connection with their Revolutionary War ancestors in the Continental army: Col. Paul Dudley Sargent and Gen. Henry Knox. Carrying studies of history to a different level, Knox recognized the fundamental connection between the past and present. Academic historians often hesitate to offer predictions about the future. In contrast, Knox viewed history as a means for examining contemporary problems, which enabled him to offer informed predictions about the future. Largely self-taught as a historian, he developed a unique approach to questions of contemporary naval strategy and maritime affairs.

Helping to expand the role of the U.S. Navy in global affairs, Knox took a historical approach in studying the strategic influence of sea power upon the military policy of the United States. Like many U.S. Navy officers of his generation, he embraced the late-nineteenth-century teachings of Alfred Thayer Mahan.[2] Exploring the challenges of professionalization within the context of American maritime strategy, global industrial revolution, and technical innovation, Mahan warned in his 1892 classic *Influence of Sea Power upon History, 1660–1783* that the U.S. Navy suffered from a "vague feeling of contempt for the past, combine[d] with natural indolence to blind men even to those strategic lessons which lie close to the surface of naval history."[3] Having considered Mahan's earlier critique at the beginning of the twentieth century, Knox encouraged fellow naval professionals to recognize that solutions to contemporary problems lay just below the surface of naval history.

The historical musings of Mahan provided the intellectual foundations for Knox to recast the U.S. Navy as an American institution with an unlimited strategic purpose. Unlike armies or air forces, he argued, warships could serve multiple missions in both peace and war. "The Navy is not merely an instrument of war," Knox argued, saying that its "role during peace is almost equally important to the nation during peace as in war."[4] Knox commanded gunboats in the Caribbean during the Spanish-American War and the Cuban insurrection, commanded warships in the Asiatic—participating in operations in the Philippines and China—and sailed the contested waters in the approaches to the Yangtze River during the Boxer Rebellion. He served with Ernest J. King and developed a similar friendship with Lt. Harry E. Yarnell during this period. King recalled that Knox encouraged wardroom explorations of the history of war, taking discussions beyond the standard interpretations of

Mahan, and introduced fellow U.S. Navy professionals to the ideas found in the writings of other great strategic thinkers, including Henri Jomini, Carl von Clausewitz, George F. R. Henderson, Spencer Wilkinson, and Julian Corbett. Reflecting upon their conversations, King described Knox as a "very accomplished and outstanding officer."[5]

Drawing from broad historical knowledge of strategic thinking, Knox challenged fellow professionals to recognize the multifaceted role of the U.S. Navy. He encouraged Navy professionals to expand their discussions of future wars to go beyond tactical operations in wartime, pressing American naval thinkers to embrace the strategic peacetime mission of avoiding future wars altogether. Using historical examples to illustrate his points, Knox sometimes ran afoul of those who favored a more tangible scientific approach using graphs and clearly outlined tables of evidence. Although few doubted his technical ability as a naval officer, some found Knox overly nostalgic about history. Capt. Roy C. Smith, for example, criticized the assertions of Knox and other junior-ranking officers who looked beyond tactics and kept pressing the strategic perspective. "It is not an economical expenditure of time for them to try and work out War College problems," he said, arguing that junior officers should recognize that their "work connected with the ship keeps them fully occupied."[6] Smith also frowned on suggestions from Knox regarding the importance of breaking the bonds of shipboard routine, reading books, and spending time on esoteric discussions of maritime affairs. Reflecting the traditional emphasis on conformity within the cloistered ranks of the service, senior officers frequently overshadowed their juniors.

Navy officers followed rules, with many riding the coattails of their superiors while navigating the path to higher command within the service. This point is highlighted in the recollections of naval officers closely affiliated with Knox. Ernest J. King, who graduated from the Naval Academy with the class of 1901, criticized the practice of indoctrinating officers to always take an empirical approach, never admit ignorance, and always place one's personal reputation ahead of other considerations. He recalled how the "average midshipman, reluctant to admit his ignorance, would stand at the blackboard chewing chalk rather than ask a question."[7] Such behavior, King suggested, was prevalent in the U.S. Navy among officers who worried more about their personal reputation than about gaining a better understanding in order to make a sound military decision.

Within the seagoing ranks of the Great White Fleet, Knox ultimately stood at the center of likeminded junior officers, in particular King. Both shared a common fascination with history. Knox explained that King had an intimate knowledge of the British admirals and Napoleon's marshals, and he later described long conversations with King about British naval heroes Sir John Jervis and Horatio Nelson. And King, Knox recalled, wore "his cap at a slight angle, kept a handkerchief in his top pocket, and often appeared with his hands in his jacket pockets," thereby emulating Fleet Admiral David Beatty, RN.[8] Knox remained a mentor to King throughout their naval careers.

Knox and King sought perspective from historical examples to develop fresh conclusions on maritime strategy and naval leadership. In particular, they traded notes from their readings about the rise of the British Empire, the Napoleonic Wars, and the American Civil War. They reveled in a particular account describing the level of devotion and blind obedience Napoleon inspired among his marshals. Upon viewing the body of Napoleon in 1840, one ninety-one-year-old marshal, Bon-Adrien Jeannot de Moncey, suddenly rose from his chair, saluted, and then fell back into his chair. In their discussions of leadership, command, and organization, Knox and King noted that the "great weakness of the Napoleonic system was that it required the detailed supervision of Napoleon." They concluded that the "lesson from the study of the Napoleonic campaigns is that you must do the opposite and train your people for independent action."[9] On questions of multinational, or combined, command, both agreed that a "lack of unity of effort results when forces of different nations, with different customs and systems of command, are brigaded together."[10]

Knox sought opportunities to escape the polished brass and white canvas that characterized life in the Great White Fleet, instead requesting assignment in the working-class navy. He specialized in smaller warships, commanding three destroyers before gaining command of the 1st Torpedo Flotilla with the rank of lieutenant. In this role, he helped organize the Atlantic Fleet in 1907. Knox remained in command as the 1st Torpedo Flotilla followed the Great White Fleet to Japan. With the establishment of the Pacific Fleet, he detached from torpedo boat command. While awaiting orders in the newly commissioned battleship USS *Nebraska* (BB 14), Knox studied the doctrinal and technical innovations of the Imperial Japanese Navy and developed a keen interest in Admiral Tōgō Heihachirō. He later equated the victory achieved by Tōgō at the 1904 Battle of Tsushima in the Tsushima Strait with that of Admiral Lord Horatio Nelson at the Battle of Trafalgar in Europe nearly one century earlier.

Fellow junior officers gravitated to Knox and King, developing a keen interest in history to gain a better understanding of the naval profession. Among others, Lt. William S. Pye became a close associate of Knox and King while serving on the Atlantic Fleet staff of Rear Adm. Hugo Osterhaus after 1911. During their time in the Osterhaus wardroom, Knox engaged King and Pye in extended discussions examining their profession. Recalling time in the flagship USS *Connecticut* (BB 18), Knox noted that "King was immensely intrigued by the memoirs of Baron de Marbot, one of Napoleon's generals and called my attention to them [and he] knew all the marshal's careers intimately."[11] In the years preceding the First World War, their studies of past wars provided firm intellectual foundations to command expeditionary operations in Latin America, maintain an American presence in Asiatic waters, and rapidly organize for wartime operations in European waters.

Knox requested assignment to the U.S. Naval War College, seeking perspective from past wars for application in contemporary operations and future U.S. Navy strategy. During his studies, he refined his ideas while working with Lt. Cdr. Arthur MacArthur III and U.S. Marine captains Earl H. "Pete" Ellis and Frederick H. Delano. The Naval War College staff included personalities deeply involved with efforts to expand the curriculum. Among other key thinkers, Knox studied with William Pratt, Frank Schofield, and William McCarty Little. Capt. William S. Sims perhaps had the greatest influence on Knox.

Sims recruited younger officers to serve in the destroyers of the Atlantic Fleet, generally based from the protected anchorage of the Narragansett Bay in Rhode Island. There, the Naval War College loomed very large as Sims continued his missionary quest to encourage his subordinates to take a broader strategic approach. He assumed duty as the commander, Destroyers, Atlantic Fleet (ComDesLant) in 1914. Afforded unique authority to select a staff, Sims arranged orders with the Bureau of Navigation to organize the ComDesLant headquarters. Among others, Sims requested Knox, King, and Pye. Thereafter, Sims nurtured a wardroom environment in which his subordinates developed new concepts of naval strategy.

Atlantic Fleet destroyers provided a practical means for Sims to experiment with tactics for maneuvering larger warships in battle. The hit-and-run tactics of destroyers and torpedo boats inspired the younger officers with Sims to break from the traditional emphasis on maintaining a structured line of battle in naval operations. Sims also anticipated the technological demise of battleships in an era of smaller and more maneuverable warships, aircraft, and submersibles. "To him all matters were clear white or dead black," King stated, recalling that while he admired "many of his ideas, [King] was never one of the group of Sims's devoted disciples and followers."[12] Later critiques of Sims and his methods note that Sims strongly encouraged junior officers serving with the Atlantic Fleet to pursue assignments to the Naval War

College. He suggested that the "War College has imbued the Navy with what we call a certain indoctrination [and] the kind of spirit that was maintained among Nelson's captains. . . . It is said that they were a band of brothers."[13] In wardroom meetings with the destroyer skippers of the Atlantic Fleet, Sims adapted the Nelsonial touch by creating a "War College afloat." He held court and presided over tabletop war games, professional discussions, and healthy debates.

Under the influence of Sims, the destroyer skippers of the Atlantic Fleet treated the works of Mahan as textbooks. Sims and his chief of staff, Capt. William Pratt, presided over the discussions. Among others, Lt. Cdr. Harold R. Stark and Lt. Cdr. William F. Halsey Jr. were frequent participants in this "War College afloat." The ideas explored at this time persisted in the minds of Knox, King, Pye, Stark, and Halsey. Often abandoning rigid procedures, they developed concepts of fluid maneuvers and coastal strikes by reading about historical naval thinkers, by joining in tabletop war games, and through practical experimentation. Sims rallied the Atlantic Fleet staff, encouraging them to reexamine questions of maritime strategy and global policy, thus providing the impetus for developing new tactics and doctrine. Sims and his Com-DesLant staff developed totally new tactics for maneuvering destroyers in unison using a wireless communications system of fewer than thirty-one words. Following the flag of Sims, the band of brothers commanding Atlantic Fleet destroyers in the shadows of the Naval War College employed their smaller warships in various scenarios for application in larger fleet operations.

The Naval Academy provided a common point of reference, although the Naval War College emerged as the focal point for higher thinking among Navy professionals. "It was at the Naval War College that Captain A. T. Mahan wrote his great works on sea power," one associate of Knox recalled, adding that the "ablest officers were all anxious to take the course at the War College, even though there were still a few die-hards who fought against it."[14] The practical education provided by Sims and the seasoning experience of the Naval War College influenced Knox to research the literary origins of U.S. Navy doctrine. From these studies, he rejected the tendency within the Navy to view war as a "process" or as a procedural exercise.

Knox criticized fellow officers who applied mathematical principles to engineering solutions rather than taking a more holistic approach in examining strategic challenges in maritime affairs. "Individually," he argued in 1915, U.S. Navy officers should be "conversant with the theory of war, and familiar with its history and the lessons derivable therefrom."[15] Roughly ten years later,

Knox lamented that the U.S. Navy had failed in its mission to serve the American taxpayers. He admonished fellow Navy professionals, telling them they were "inherently responsible that its citizens are duly informed upon matters which affect their broader interests, and which in the final analysis they must decide."[16] Knox criticized Navy leaders for being willfully ignorant of this basic responsibility, "largely due to glaring deficiencies in our written naval history, which in their turn arise from the extraordinary inaccessibility of authentic sources."[17]

Questions of strategy and naval command fell within the context of lessons derived from the past. For Knox, historical studies provided foundations for engendering an underlying spirit of professionalism within the U.S. Navy ranks—from the lowest seaman to the highest ranking leaders within the chain of command. By extension, Knox engaged American taxpayers by orchestrating an unbridled propaganda campaign designed to justify the realization of a "Two Ocean Navy" and "Navy Second to None." His writings reflected a potent brew of heroic interpretations of America's maritime past combined with contemporary discussions about the crucial functions of the Navy as a *national* institution of the United States. Knox served as the trusted advisor of key personalities within the service, including Sims, Pye, Yarnell, Stark, King, Edward C. Kalbfus, and William D. Leahy. Within the ranks, Knox spearheaded the intellectual charge in framing a strategic argument for the Navy to pursue operations beyond the American hemisphere. In turn he suggested that a "strong Navy is needed for trade protection, not only when we may possibly be at war, but also more probably and more often when we are a peaceful neutral."[18]

Emergent Historian at War

The British Empire inspired American conceptions of sea power and strategic discussions about the U.S. Navy mission in global maritime affairs. The Royal Navy also provided one model by which to expand the U.S. Navy in anticipation of the twentieth century. Given their basic technical training as engineers and able seamen, American naval officers widely referred to Mahan in addressing fundamental flaws embedded within the educational curriculum of the Naval Academy and within the enlisted ranks of the U.S. Navy. At the Naval War College, the works of Mahan remained central references. The curriculum also featured ideas derived from the earlier works of Sir John Knox Laughton and Rear Adm. Stephen B. Luce.[19] Great military thinkers and the literary classics of war added spice to discussions among U.S. Navy professionals in examining the inherent challenges of strategy, tactics, and command.

In particular, Knox found inspiration in the historical writings of Naval War College founders Luce and Mahan. Both remained actively engaged in the effort to continue an intellectual revolution within the ranks of the Navy. Mahan and Luce were aware of officers like Knox from reading those officers' articles in the U.S. Naval Institute *Proceedings*. Mahan died suddenly in 1914 and Luce passed away in 1917, and during this period, Knox took it upon himself to follow in their footsteps by expanding strategic connections between the Naval War College and the Navy Department.

The Naval War College inspired radical organizational changes within the Navy Department, which extended to the seagoing ranks of the Navy. Knox drew from experimental concepts developed at the Naval War College to organize the Office of Chief of Naval Operations (CNO) in 1915. He concurrently assumed a leadership role on the newly established Operations Navy (OpNav) staff. Under the CNO, the OpNav staff included the Office of Naval Intelligence (ONI), which received the administrative designation of "Op-16." Within the ONI, Knox created the Historical Section under the designation of "Op-16-E." Knox created a direct relationship between the academic studies of maritime strategy at the Naval War College and the practical focus of the ONI in efforts to coordinate naval operations with intelligence. Wireless and aviation technologies changed the traditional relationship between headquarters ashore and warships at sea. In efforts to develop fresh doctrinal means to harness the advantages of new technology, Knox continued working from within the ONI to assist Sims in efforts to encourage professionalization within the ranks, synthesize Navy command, and develop an American navy second to none. With his promotion to rear admiral in 1917, Sims briefly assumed duty as president of the Naval War College.

The American declaration of war against the Central Powers fueled fresh debates within the U.S. Navy, which hinged upon defining the wartime role of the CNO in orchestrating seagoing operations. Given the global scope of American maritime strategy, the CNO, Adm. William S. Benson, selected the Naval War College president, Sims, to act under Benson's authority as representative to the American Expeditionary Forces (AEF) in Europe. The limitations of transatlantic communications at the time required Sims to sail to London with orders to act on behalf of the CNO in negotiating relations with foreign governments, Allied headquarters, other agencies of the U.S. government, and the U.S. Army. To fulfill these responsibilities, Sims recruited Knox to join his staff, which was installed at Grosvenor Gardens in central London by April 1917. Following the Royal Navy tradition of naming buildings after historic ships, Sims referred to the "stone frigate" housing the U.S. Navy headquarters as the "London Flagship."

Acting under the general authority of the CNO in London, Sims frequently struggled to safeguard U.S. Navy interests while negotiating combined maritime strategy with foreign allies. Operations hinged upon an efficient system of intelligence collaboration among the Allied navies. To these ends, Sims placed Knox in charge of fusing U.S. Navy operations with intelligence. Within the London Flagship, Knox created the Planning Section to empower Sims in dealings with the Royal Navy as well as coordinate U.S. Navy operations on the European front. "The business of the 'Planning Section,'" Sims later explained, "was to make studies of particular problems, to prepare plans for future operations, and also to criticize fully the organization and methods which were already in existence." Sims empowered Knox and the Planning Section to "place themselves in the position of the Germans and to decide how, if they were directing German naval operations, they would frustrate the tactics of the Allies."[20] Upon arrival on the European warfront in April 1917, Knox sought personnel with suitable experience for service in the Planning Section.

The culture within the service left the U.S. Navy unprepared to claim an equal place within the multinational Anglo-French alliance. In the U.S. Navy, personnel offering technical expertise in seagoing operations frequently overshadowed those specializing in other, perhaps less tangible, fields within the service. Line officers generally focused on operations, marginalizing the potential role of fellow naval officers assigned to "special duty" in the fields of communications or intelligence.[21] Recalling the prevailing culture within the Navy, one contemporary suggested that "everybody sort of thought Naval Intelligence was striped pants, cookie-pushers, going to parties and so on."[22] Another noted that "intelligence can produce nothing tangible in peace time." The ONI "was in time of peace an office that did not draw the best talent in the Navy," he argued. "Officers who went into it generally got left by the wayside," and "with a few exceptions they were largely not the best."[23]

Royal Navy officers shared similar biases against specialists affiliated with new technical fields, such as communications and intelligence. During the First World War, the Admiralty addressed this problem by recruiting civilian volunteers into the reserve ranks of the Royal Navy. By 1915 the Admiralty had established a centralized headquarters to fuse seagoing operations with intelligence. Within its Naval Intelligence Division (NID), "Room 40" provided information derived from enemy communications. This information provided crucial insights for Royal Navy strategists in the effort to understand and anticipate the movements of enemy forces at the front. Upon arriving in 1917, Sims wanted to establish a similar organization inside the London Flagship. In turn he empowered Knox to solicit the Bureau of Navigation for additional personnel with specialized expertise in communications and intelligence.

Drawing from the Royal Navy solution to expand the communications and intelligence ranks, Knox recruited American civilians for temporary wartime duty in the London Flagship. Among others, there was Tracy Barrett Kittredge, who studied history and literature at the University of California at Berkley. During his studies he participated in the California Naval Militia and afterward attended Exeter College at the University of Oxford. An American expatriate in Europe at the beginning of the First World War, Kittredge also worked as director of the Education Fund under Herbert Hoover on the Commission for Relief in Belgium. His fluency in French and German provided additional expertise, which the U.S. Navy immediately requested within the London Flagship. With additional endorsements from Cdr. Harold R. Stark in the Operations Division and Cdr. John V. Babcock in the Naval Intelligence Division of the London Flagship, Knox nominated Kittredge for a civil service appointment. In turn, Vice Adm. Sims arranged a reserve commission for Kittredge. As a result, he was among the first to receive a line officer's commission with the rank of lieutenant (jg) in the U.S. Navy Auxiliary Volunteer Reserve.

Knox and Kittredge established a lasting bureaucratic alliance in their mutual campaign to fuse U.S. Navy operations with the intelligence derived from the broader understanding of history. During the First World War, Knox relied heavily upon Kittredge as a London Flagship liaison. Through Kittredge, Knox also fostered personal ties with Frank Birch and Alfred "Dilly" Knox (no relation) within the Naval Intelligence Division's Subsection 25 (NID-25) at the Admiralty. Sims recalled that "throughout the war Kittredge's previous historical training, European experience, and fine intellectual gifts made his services very valuable in the Intelligence Department."[24] Given access to high-grade sources, Knox and Kittredge filtered information to the Operations Subsection of the London Flagship, which was under Cdr. John V. Babcock and Cdr. Harold R. Stark. In turn the London Flagship supplied information to the Atlantic Fleet headquarters of Adm. Henry T. Mayo. The chief of staff at the Atlantic Fleet, Knox's old friend Capt. Ernest J. King, helped disseminate information supplied by the London Flagship to facilitate U.S. Navy operations in European waters.

Because the Admiralty and Navy Department lacked formally defined procedures for coordinating combined operations, Anglo-American intelligence collaboration on the European front centered on informal gentlemen's agreements. The chain of command within the U.S. Navy also lacked clarity, as Adm. William S. Benson pioneered efforts to establish the authority of the CNO in relation to subordinate commanders ashore and afloat. U.S. Army and Navy commanders struggled to collaborate in organizing the AEF during the First World War. Similarly, the Royal Navy and U.S. Navy struggled to establish clear relationships among various headquarters ashore and afloat. By 1918 Knox and the Planning Section of the London Flagship had provided a means to overcome the problems of combined and joint command. As the U.S. Navy lacked formal intelligence training for line officers, Knox also relied heavily upon civilian historians like Kittredge who were serving in the reserve ranks.

Civilian scholars on reserve service helped nurture collegial relations between British and American naval intelligence staffs. The British organization included a large number of reserve officers and civilian scholars associated with the Historical Section of NID, which had been established with the recommendation of Sir Julian Corbett under the approval of Winston S. Churchill as the first sea lord. Prewar connections with Dilly Knox and Birch enhanced the influence of Kittredge inside the London Flagship. Behind closed doors, the London Flagship staff set precedence for lasting collaboration between the Admiralty and Navy Department. As the leading member of the Planning Section, Knox recognized that the allied navies drew from centuries of experience in global maritime affairs.

The AEF forces had to adapt in order to collaborate with various strategic Anglo-French headquarters on the European front. The Royal Navy ultimately assumed operational command over U.S. Navy forces in the embattled waters and ashore on the railroads and in the trenches. American commanders retained tactical control, but they often questioned orders issued by foreign allies. This experience greatly influenced the perspectives of U.S. Navy veterans of the European campaign. Under pressure from the Anglo-French allies, American forces participated in the campaign against Bolshevik insurgents in Russia after 1917. In a letter to Sims, Churchill, then the British minister of munitions, described the adventure to Siberia as the cornerstone for future transatlantic collaboration between the British and American navies. Churchill applauded Sims for the "cordial terms, which in laying down the command of U.S. Naval Forces in European waters, you convey your recognition and zeal with which we have endeavored."[25]

Having experienced the problems of combined command, Knox helped mitigate friction between the London Flagship and other U.S. Navy staffs on the European front. Along with Stark in the London Flagship, Knox engaged personal connections with King and Pye, key members of the Atlantic Fleet staff. Drawing from their First World War experiences, Knox, King, and Pye recommended a new educational strategy for the postwar U.S. Navy. They understood the importance of differentiating training, rote memorization, and doctrinal procedure from the pursuit of a broadly humanistic approach to the sciences, literature, and history. "Book learning, abstract knowledge, is like fertilizer," they argued. "It does not, of itself, produce anything, but it stimulates growth and advance when the live seed, practical experience, is instilled into the soil." Continuing, they observed that the "naval profession is the most varied in the world. . . . The naval officer required a working knowledge of many branches of human endeavor."[26]

With the Allied victory in Europe, Sims returned to the Naval War College and overhauled the curriculum to improve the educational foundations of the U.S. Navy. Again he recruited Kittredge and Knox for assistance. By 1920 Kittredge was serving as the archivist at the Naval War College. In this role, he expanded the Naval War College library and research collection—helping in the effort to expand the educational curriculum for the study of past wars. He also assisted Sims in drafting his memoir, *The Victory at Sea*. Driving home points that Sims had to avoid for the sake of political decorum, Kittredge leveled a highly critical analysis of the Navy Department administration in his 1921 study, *Naval Lessons of the Great War*. About the same time, Sims assembled a board comprised of Knox, King, and Pye, who drew lessons from their experiences in the First World War to produce the definitive "Report and Recommendations of a Board Appointed by the Bureau of Navigation Regarding the Instruction and Training of Line Officers." The board determined that U.S. Navy officers generally suffered from an adolescent approach to questions of war and peace as a result of being " 'educated' only in preparation for the lowest commissioned grade."[27]

Broadening the educational curriculum for American naval personnel provided an essential advantage for those charged with assuming positions of leadership ashore and at sea. The recommendations of the Knox-King-Pye board largely served as the foundation for conditioning U.S. Navy personnel during the interwar period. Knox also assisted the Naval War College president, Rear Adm. Edward C. Kalbfus, in writing the U.S. Navy planning manual, *Sound Military Decision*. In this work, the Navy officially refuted Army doctrine, which emphasized "principles of war," arguing that the "condensation of the fundamentals of war, [have] been known to cause confusion and to result in failure to recognize the principles which are intended to be brought to mind." Among other points, Knox and Kalbfus cautioned students to recognize fundamental differences between military operations ashore and naval operations afloat.[28]

To achieve objectives ashore, navies had the capacity to provide leverage for diplomatic negotiation. Unlike land-oriented armies or air forces, the maritime focus of navies provided unique means to secure national interests in peacetime without having to engage in war. In lectures, Knox invoked the founder of the Naval War College, Rear Adm. Stephen Luce, by suggesting that "all naval operations are strategic."

"Quasi" Wars

After the First World War, bureaucratic rivalry characterized relations between the War Department and the Navy Department, and that rivalry passed into the ranks of the Army and Navy. Knox directly participated in these feudal battles. He fused debates surrounding the influence of sea power with those concerning the future military policy of the United States. On his formal retirement from active service in October 1921, Knox continued to follow this basic course. From 1922 he served in retired naval status as director of the Office of Navy Records and Library at the Navy Department. In this role, Knox fused historical research with practical discussions surrounding the focus of U.S. Navy strategy.

Airpower enthusiasts within the War Department competed for control over aviation, as the Navy Department examined aircraft carrier and zeppelin technology. Centralization in aviation had defined British policy after the First World War, and the Royal Air Force provided one model by which U.S. Army Air Corps officers envisioned a separate air force designed to consolidate Army and Navy aviation. Col. William "Billy" Mitchell, USA, took a particularly outspoken stand on the question of unifying the aviation branches of the Army and Navy under the vision of strategic airpower. He pressed his points in the media and openly challenged higher-ranking superiors and politicians, which resulted in his widely publicized court-martial in 1925. He subsequently nurtured his reputation as a bureaucratic martyr in efforts to develop American strategic airpower policy. Having assisted Mitchell within the Army, Maj. Henry "Hap" Arnold helped draft Field Manual 100-20, *Command and Employment of Air Power,* the first page of which emphasizes that "land power and air power are co-equal and interdependent forces; neither is the auxiliary for the other. . . . Air power may be properly and profitably employed against enemy sea power, land power, and air power."[29]

Strategic efforts by aviators to escape the tactical constraints of the land-oriented U.S. Army carried implications for the U.S. Navy, which sought control over the development of airpower in the maritime arena. The fight for air ultimately defined bureaucratic relations between the War Department and Navy Department. Knox referred to historical precedence to refute arguments about the "new" challenges of technology. He also criticized the emphasis on warship tonnage within the Navy in his 1922 study, *Eclipse of American Sea Power.* "A navy whose personnel is really efficient may easily be twice as strong actually as another of equal paper strength in ships but whose personnel is only moderately efficient," Knox argued. He concluded that "history affords many striking examples" regarding the "influence of efficient personnel in multiplying the power of material."[30] Although the service also required specialized technical expertise, he viewed the retired and reserve ranks as the best source from which the Navy could draw specialists into the regular line ranks as needed.

Knox embraced fiscal realities as an opportunity to organize the U.S. Navy into an elite cadre of dedicated professionals. Holding the line on active service in peacetime, the Navy had the capacity to draw from the retired and reserve ranks on an as-required basis in wartime. The Navy required seagoing professionals capable of performing the basic maritime constabulary mission of navigating the complicated legal waters between peace and war. Noting that the "supreme test of the naval strategist is the depth of his comprehension of the intimate relation between sea power and land power, and of the truth that all effort afloat should be directed at an effect ashore," Knox warned that history "abounds in examples of naval effort misdirected because the naval mission was too restricted in its military outlook."[31]

Knox portrayed the Navy as the service that most closely reflected the vision of the founding fathers in safeguarding the global maritime interests of the United States. He exploited the heroic reputation of George Washington to provide an apparently neutral point of historical reference for American readers, and he capitalized on the mythology surrounding the Franco-American campaign against the British at Yorktown in 1781, which fueled the Sesquicentennial Celebration on the historic battlefield in 1931. Herbert Hoover and future president Franklin D. Roosevelt spoke at the event.[32]

During his speech, Roosevelt noted the importance of American influence within the global context of economic revitalization. Naval influence, coupled with the repeal of Prohibition, stood at the center of the Roosevelt agenda. In 1932 Knox published his second book, *The Naval Genius of George Washington.* Having earned positive reviews, Knox received an invitation to discuss his work with Roosevelt. Following a series of meetings at Hyde Park in New York and on Campobello Island in the Canadian province of New Brunswick, the two developed a very close alliance in efforts to fuse domestic New Deal policies with a two-ocean Navy strategy of deterrence.

Roosevelt framed global strategy on the basic concept of employing the Navy in operations designed to defend critical American economic interests. To these ends, he assumed the role of patron for Knox. In turn the assertions in Knox's writings reflected the domestic agenda of the Roosevelt administration during the 1930s. "The over-maligned pacifist is entitled to much respect and consideration," Knox observed, suggesting that despite "limitations of the Navy Department . . . there are many opportunities for officers as individuals, too frequently avoided, for direct contact with the people through the press and the platform."[33] In this debate, Knox suggested Navy leaders should frame discussions of the military policy of the United States within the objective context of the past. He argued that discussions of American maritime strategy suffered "due to a lack of understanding of the fact that the Navy is not merely an instrument of war," explaining that "its role during peace is almost equally important to the nation during peace as in war. Like the Constitution, the function of the navy is multiple."[34]

As a retired Navy officer, Knox drew from firsthand experience to frame compelling historical arguments to rally American readers. He gained wide attention among academic historians, including Princeton University professor Edward Meade Earle and Harvard University professors Robert Greenhalgh Albion and Samuel Eliot Morison. Unlike academic historians, however, Knox wrote with unique authority on Navy operations of the past and present. For this reason, Franklin Delano Roosevelt commissioned Knox in 1934 to write official histories of the U.S. Navy. The president diverted funds appropriated under legislation sponsored by Georgia congressman Carl Vinson and Florida congressman Park Trammell to finance Knox's historical research. In a bipartisan effort to expand the Navy, they passed the Vinson-Trammell Act of 1934, but this legislation was intended for the purposes of developing weapons and warships. Roosevelt justified the use of Vinson-Trammell funding to finance Knox's historical work under the general concept of advancing the education of U.S. Navy professionals by helping them better understand concepts of maritime strategy through studying the influence of sea power on history.

Roosevelt insisted upon beginning the series with a volume examining the obscure origins of the U.S. Navy and its undeclared role in the wars against France and the Barbary pirates. At first Knox disagreed with this approach, but he recognized the strategic thinking behind Roosevelt's idea after submitting the proposed title for the multivolume project, "History of the War with France, 1798–1801." (Roosevelt changed the title to *The Quasi-War with France*.)[35] Knox understood how Roosevelt intended to engage American readers about the future focus of U.S. Navy operations after 1937. Roosevelt and Knox agreed that navies were fundamentally unlike other military services and branches of government. Unlike the Army, the Navy remained actively engaged in warlike operations in peacetime while safeguarding maritime lines of global economic communications.

Using American shipyards as another means to address the economic depression in the 1930s, Roosevelt employed the Navy as the first line of defense against foreign aggressors in Asia and Europe. By 1934, Imperial Japanese forces had begun to threaten American interests in Asiatic waters. Likewise, National Socialist Germany and Fascist Italy undermined stability in European affairs. "Truly the time has come for American education and indoctrination in maritime matters," Knox wrote, suggesting the need for "a national awakening in the major play of national economic forces which inevitably link up production, sea transportation, foreign markets and sources of materials with naval power." He concluded that a "strong Navy is needed for trade protection, not only when we may possibly be at war, but also more probably and more often when we are a peaceful neutral."[36]

Relevance of History

Knox challenged fellow naval professionals to recognize the inherent relevance of history in examining contemporary problems. In his writings, Knox cited historical examples when strategists foolishly anticipated the unknown future without first pursuing a detailed understanding of the past. Largely self-taught as a historian, he relied upon the scholarly advice of academic scholars such as Earle, Morison, and Albion. Among other key allies, Roosevelt, Stark, King, and Kittredge remained heavily involved with Knox and his work in framing the American strategy of neutrality in anticipation of the Second World War. Knox assisted in charting a course through the uncertain waters of neutrality between 1939 and 1941. After the Pearl Harbor disaster, Knox once again recruited civilians with formal training as historians to serve within the intel-ligence subdivisions of the Navy. Twenty years after entering the civil service at the Navy Department, following the Japanese attack on Pearl Harbor in 1941, Knox reported for duty in uniform as a U.S. Navy captain in a retired status. In this role, he continued working behind the scenes as an advisor to Roosevelt, Stark, and King during the Second World War.

Roosevelt consulted with Knox when making many key decisions, among them reorganizing the Navy for global operations. The division of authorities between the CNO and the commander in chief, U.S. Navy (ComInCh), had contributed to problems before 1941, but Roosevelt resolved this division of power under congressional war powers through Executive Orders 8984 and 9096. Knox also influenced Roosevelt to install King as the preeminent U.S. Navy strategist and operational commander after 1942. His unified headquar-ters inside the Main Navy complex in Washington, D.C., ultimately served as the center of global Anglo-American operations and intelligence. This point is clearly reflected within the text of the recently digitized "Graybook" of Adm. Chester W. Nimitz, written while he was commander in chief, Pacific Ocean Area.[37] His running "Estimate of the Situation" consistently shows the strategic hand of King in relation to the decisions Nimitz acted upon in orchestrating operations in the Pacific theater.

Knox recruited civilian historians serving in reserve status at the Navy Department to produce operational assessments. Afforded unique access to operational messages, key commanders, and "combat intelligence" sources, Knox and his historians pioneered methods in operational "decision analy-sis."[38] Historians affiliated with Knox included Earle, Morison, and Albion. Their students also served in reserve status as Navy officers under the overall supervision of Knox. With help from others, James A. Michener, Walter Muir Whitehill, and Elting E. Morison helped Knox produce the "postmortem" reports of recent battles. These unpublished wartime histories later directly influenced the conclusions found within semiofficial works by Samuel Eliot Morison after the Second World War.

British perspectives provide useful insight into the influence of Knox on the questions of command within the U.S. Navy's conception of sea power. For example, Captain Alfred C. Dewar, RN, supervised the Historical Section within the Training and Staff Division of the Admiralty. As earlier discussed, the Admiralty drew personnel from the Historical Section to organize their wartime Operational Intelligence Center and other NID analytical subsec-tions. On the other side of the Atlantic, Dewar's organization inspired Knox to create an equivalent within the Navy Department. In June 1944, Secretary of the Navy James V. Forrestal empowered CNO/CominCh King to establish the Office of Naval History (ONH) under the president of the Naval War College, Adm. Edward C. Kalbfus. The Naval War College mission coincided with the new role of ONH, which had "authority to coordinate histories and narratives shall include the history of operations being prepared by Commander S.E. Morison, USNR, the administrative history under Dr. R. G. Albion, the Battle reports of the Office of Public Relations, the record of aviation accomplishment, and the Combat Narratives of the Office of Naval Intelligence."[39]

Kalbfus focused on strategy while Knox supervised the daily operations within ONH. Under the overall authorities of CNO/CominCh, Knox organized the ONH to provide direct support to U.S. Naval operations. He simultaneously contributed to the work performed by the Naval War College and ONI. Greatly impressed, Dewar explained to the Admiralty that "Knox possessed authority comparable to that of the First Lord."[40]

In the following essays, readers will revisit the writings of Knox to examine themes found in more recent debates surrounding the role of American sea power. Knox criticized the bureaucratic tradition of micromanagement within the U.S. Navy and rallied fellow naval professionals to avoid blind obedience. He also found that the Navy essentially fell into an intellectual rut with the unification of the American armed forces after the Second World War. Although it is impossible to know whether Knox would agree, it is clear from his writings that he would likely find fundamental problems in contemporary American strategy and policy. In his time, the Imperial Japanese Navy and the Royal Navy served as the foils for U.S. Navy strategic planning. Yet strategic war plans centered on American efforts to maintain technical and doctrinal advantages over foreign navies.

For Knox, all naval operations in peacetime remained a strategic element in broader efforts to avoid future wars. In this respect, he shared a similar perspective with other strategic thinkers after the Second World War, including George F. Kennan, Professor Herbert Rosinski, and U.S. Navy rear admirals Joseph C. Wylie and Stansfield Turner. Unlike the orientation of land forces to seize and hold territory or the destructive nature of strategic bombing theorists, Knox emphasized the flexible nature of navies to transcend the nexus between strategy and tactics. Maritime thinkers, he believed, required strategic understanding of past wars in order to assert command over tactical forces in future battles.

Many of the essays found in the following collection originally appeared in the *Proceedings* of the U.S. Naval Institute between 1913 and 1950. The original manuscripts frequently featured unique annotations and correspondence between Knox, his publishers, and professional associates. Thus this work includes material derived from archival collections featuring the original papers of Knox located at the Library of Congress, the U.S. Naval Academy Nimitz Library, the U.S. Naval War College, and the Franklin D. Roosevelt Presidential Library and Archives. Knox also maintained a healthy correspondence with foreign associates whose papers are located at the Churchill College Archives near Cambridge, the British National Archives at Kew, and the Liddell Hart Library at King's College in London. To preserve the original intentions of Knox and to avoid misinterpretation, several sentences with unclear syntax have been reproduced as they originally appeared at the time of publication. For this reason, editorial changes have been kept to an absolute minimum, and readers may notice some inconsistencies in grammar, usage, and style.

The 21st Century Foundations series of the Naval Institute Press follows a proud tradition that asks contemporary American thinkers to revisit the ideas of luminaries from the past in order to address strategic questions of contemporary and future importance. With these thoughts in mind, I have kept the introductory narratives to the original Knox essays to a minimum so readers can treat his essays as introductory primers to his broader works on questions of maritime strategy, naval leadership, and historical scholarship. Indeed, Knox offers some very provocative observations from the first fifty years of the twentieth century that resonate within the context of the twenty-first.

ONE

Marching to the Sound of Guns

ontinuing wardroom traditions dating from the age of sail,
U.S. Navy professionals of Knox's generation engaged in
spirited debates about the relationship between strategy
and tactics, which seemed more complicated within the context of
technology in an age increasingly characterized by warships of
steam and steel. Knox used the semiofficial forum provided by the
U.S. Naval Institute's *Proceedings* to highlight new ideas. He initially
drafted papers for presentation within the wardroom aboard ship
while also preparing essays for presentation before fellow students
at the Naval War College. Refining his ideas in discussions with
shipmates at sea, Knox earned wide notoriety within Navy ranks
for publishing the prize-winning essay in the March 1913 issue of
Proceedings. The essay, "Trained Initiative and Unity of Action: The
True Bases of Military Efficiency," addressed the question of naval
leadership by emphasizing the importance of delegation.

Knox strongly criticized U.S. Navy leaders for taking a lazy
approach to command by micromanaging subordinates through
administrative procedures and assigning them the most mundane
of tasks. He addressed the problem of technology, emphasizing
the importance of taking a broader view in understanding the universal principles of strategy and tactics in maritime operations.
Knox and his close associate, Ernest J. King, highlighted the writings of Alfred Thayer Mahan and Julian Corbett in published
essays, written orders, and professional conversations. As an editor
for *Proceedings*, King encouraged Knox to build upon the ideas
found in "Trained Initiative and Unity of Action." In 1914 Knox

expanded upon the essay's basic principles by providing historical analogies in two additional *Proceedings* articles, "The Great Lesson from Nelson for Today" and "Old Principles and Modern Applications." Examining the unique challenges inherent in naval leadership, Knox used historical examples such as British naval hero Admiral Lord Horatio Nelson and his American equivalent, Commo. John Paul Jones, to articulate deeper points on transcendent questions of contemporary interest for fellow U.S. Navy professionals and strategic thinkers. He also used historical analogies to rally American taxpayers in peacetime to recognize the naval services as the first defender of the United States in wartime.[1]

Knox challenged ranking Navy readers to abandon the practice of focusing on administration by encouraging them to avoid micromanagement. He also criticized those who tended toward using a mathematical approach to questions of war and the "concentration on fractions." In the following essay, Knox leveled a full broadside with the observation that the prevailing Navy "system of highly centralized authority renders it necessary to issue lengthy orders covering a great number of details." In what was for Knox an ongoing theme, he pressed readers to embrace the concept of the initiative of the subordinate. For his more provocative points, Knox paraphrased other authors to encourage discussion within the U.S. Navy ranks. In examining the challenges of naval command, he drew heavily from the writings of Germany's Field Marshal Helmuth von Moltke and Britain's Colonel George F. R. Henderson. "Intelligent cooperation," Knox argued, is of "infinitely more value than mechanical obedience."[2] The following essay appeared at the dawn of the twentieth century, but the ideas articulated by Knox resonate today, as U.S. Navy leaders have frequently visited similar questions in the twenty-first century.

TRAINED INITIATIVE AND UNITY OF ACTION: THE TRUE BASES OF MILITARY EFFICIENCY

1913

Motto: *Concert in action makes strength.*
Jomini

Introductory

In summing up his justly famed work on the *Operations of War*, [Edward Bruce] Hamley makes an analysis of what he calls the "primary factors which have always been the foundation of success." According to this venerated authority there are two "indispensable factors": first, good morale (in which an approximate equality may in the future be expected among civilized nations), and second, a good commander. After the two indispensable factors, next in order are "mobility, combination and firepower." "Mobility is spoken of here in the tactical sense—meaning rapidity of maneuvers on the battlefield"; firepower needs no comment.

It is the purpose of this paper to treat only [the power] of combination, which, in the military sense, is the power to accomplish the will of the commander through the coordinated efforts of the several units of the command. [Henri] Jomini says the "guiding principle in tactical combinations, as in those of strategy, is to bring the mass of the force in hand against a part of the opposing army, and upon that point the possession of which promises the most important results." This then, in general terms, will be the aim underlying the dispositions of the commander, but it will not alone be sufficient for him to will (or even to order) a certain course of action; there must exist within the organization the mechanism of putting that will into effect—a means of overcoming the friction which is inherent in all operations involving the coordinated effort, the concerted action, of a large number of men or units. To once more quote Hamley, "combination depends on the efficiency of the chain of control connecting the brain of the commander through all grades down to the corporal's guard, on the intelligence of subordinate readers in grasping and applying the commander's plans, on the discipline which insures intelligent obedience to the directing will, and on the mobility which gives rapid effect to that will and permits of fleeting opportunities being taken advantage of."

In operations preliminary to and in those succeeding a fleet engagement, the naval forces are usually widely scattered. The parts comprise single ships (scouting and doing other miscellaneous duty) and groups composed of scouts, screening forces, main body and train; between which, as well as between the forces afloat and the shore establishment, careful coordination is manifestly necessary. In addition to strategic and administrative coordination, it requires no great stretch of the professional imagination to appreciate in a general way the concert of effort that will be even more necessary, and far more difficult of attainment, in the field of tactics. There will be fast wing attacks on the flanks; destroyer threats and destroyer attacks, supported by cruiser groups; submarine and mining threats and attacks; torpedo threats and attacks by heavy ships; and changes of course, speed and formation. Not only must our own movements be planned and executed, but those of the enemy must be comprehended and met. Large groups of all classes will break up into smaller groups, and these again into still smaller ones; ships will often find themselves isolated; formations will be ragged; and confusion will frequently arise. All will happen within a few minutes—perhaps less than an hour will decide the action.

The fate of a battle is the happening of an instant. A decisive moment arrives when the smallest act decides and gives superiority.

In such a kaleidoscopic drama initiative and decision of the highest order will be almost continuously demanded of commanders, from the highest to the lowest. If each independent action, each hasty decision, fails to serve the plan of the commander-in-chief; if his will does not guide the ever changing situations, great and small, to seize fleeting opportunities, to ward off threatened disaster, and to comply with the guiding principles of tactics as interpreted by himself: then the various commanders will work at cross-purposes, the action of one will neither support nor be supported by the action of another, and whatever is accomplished will be only negative. If fortunate, serious disorder among the fleet may be avoided while carrying on a purely passive "hammer and tongs" column fight; but no brilliant tactics nor decisive results can be hoped for; a spark of genius may flicker here and there, but will not survive its isolation.

To provide against humiliation and disaster, it seems imperative to supplement the present inadequate means for administering our affairs during peace or war, and for carrying on both strategic operations and fleet engagements. Neither signals, radio-messages, nor instructions, written or verbal, can suffice, either singly or in combination, to produce the unity of effort—the concert of action—demanded by modern conditions in a large fleet. Until this need is filled—a new means furnished—an able commander and a fleet possessing high morale, good mobility and great firepower, are in a measure wasted, since the power of combination is lacking. The skillful admiral will not have the means of using effectively his well-wrought instrument.

The necessity for and the difficulty of efficient coordination within a large force operating against an enemy being recognized, it will be interesting to examine into the methods of some of the greatest military leaders, to see how they solved this difficulty, and then finally to compare their methods with those now existing in our own naval service.

The Methods of Great Men

Napoleon's method of field management consisted primarily of detailed instructions which aimed to foresee and provide for variations due to the movements of the enemy, accidents, the weather and other variable factors. It depended for success upon the care and skill with which the instructions were prepared and upon rigid obedience of the same to the letter. Realizing its weakness, though not having sufficiently long intervals of peace to prepare and substitute a better method, the great Frenchman supplemented it, when possible, by personal supervision of important operations; and, when long and close association with a marshal warranted it an exception would be made and only general instructions would be issued to him. During a battle each situation, as it presented itself, was handled by verbal messages transmitted through mounted staff officers.

Napoleon's campaigns were conspicuously successful when the operations were small enough to permit his personal direction at every critical point. His genius was then of use wherever required. During one of the early Italian campaigns he constantly employed himself without sleep or rest for five days and nights. Those early Italian campaigns are by far the most brilliant in history, and, as is generally conceded, the only ones ever conducted by a commander without a single error of strategy or tactics.

Following Napoleon's military career it becomes plainly evident that, as the magnitude of the operations increased, his success diminished directly. Unless he himself could personally oversee and supervise operations, his system fell to pieces. This is conspicuously true of the Russian campaign and those succeeding it in Germany, where the numbers engaged and the fields of operation were very large. Examples occur of brilliant work on the part of his marshals acting independently; rarely, however, except when taking part in the same general campaign with Napoleon himself and when the marshal so acting was a pupil of long standing. Long and close association in the field had taught these what action they could expect from the Emperor under most circumstances, as well as what he expected from them.

His disasters, beginning with the Russian campaign and culminating at Leipzig, and again at Waterloo, must be attributed in part to the losses through wounds, death, or disaffection of such able and well-trained marshals as Lannes, Murat, Massena, and Augereau. Napoleon's system of centralization demanded, for success in large operations, lieutenants of long personal association. Napoleon himself, at St. Helena, in criticizing certain of his marshals, frequently said that certain ones failed "because he did not understand my system." This in itself indicates that there could have been no other system except that of highly centralized authority, unsupplemented by any other school than that of war itself under the master.

Nelson and von Moltke each used a method far superior to that of Napoleon for producing coordination or "combination." It consisted primarily, in the issuing of general instructions only, but was in each case supplemented by a thoroughly worked out and clearly understood system of command, and by unity of doctrine.

Nelson's own conduct at the battle of Cape St. Vincent is well known and is a conspicuous illustration of initiative taken without instructions. In commenting upon this action Mahan says, "the justification of departure from orders lies not in success but in the conditions of the case; Jervis was not one to overlook these, nor thereafter to forget that only one man in his fleet had both seen the thing to do and dared the responsibility of doing it." In regard to Nelson's methods Mahan states as follows: "Upon his own subordinates Nelson laid a distinct charge that he should expect them to use their judgment and act upon it with independence, sure of his generous construction and support of their action." Again, commenting on Nelson's famous memorandum before the battle of Trafalgar, Mahan says that it "is memorable not only for the sagacity and comprehensiveness of its general dispositions, but even more for the magnanimous confidence with which the details of execution were freely entrusted to those upon whom they had to fall." Probably the most striking illustration of all is Mahan's comment upon the famous signal before going into action at Trafalgar, as follows: "It is said that Collingwood, frequently testy and at the moment preoccupied with the approaching collision, exclaimed impatiently when the first number went aloft, 'I wish Nelson would stop signaling, as we know well enough what we have to do!'"

While the principles under which Nelson commanded his fleet were the same as those of von Moltke, to the latter is due the credit of the widespread and detailed application of those principles throughout a large army.

In 1870, after only a few weeks of war, Germany, but a newcomer among the powers, had laid France, the once all powerful, prostrate. Europe and all the world were undisguisedly astounded. To what were these unprecedented results due? The numbers were about equal on each side. At the end of July the numbers were: German, 384,000; French, 250,000. By the middle of November they were: German, 425,000; French, 600,000. Germany had no advantage in the morale or discipline of her troops; the French commanders were the more experienced in war; the firepower, mobility, and all other factors but one, were about equal in the two armies. The Germans far excelled the French only in the *power of combination*. To quote Colonel Henderson:

> It was understood, therefore, in the Prussian armies of 1866 and 1870 that no order was to be blindly obeyed unless the superior who issued it was actually present, and therefore cognizant of the situation at the time it was received. If this was not the case, the recipient was to use his own judgment, and act as he believed his superior would have directed him to do had he been aware how matters stood. Again, officers not in direct communication with headquarters were expected not only to watch for and utilize, on their own initiative, all opportunities of furthering the plan of campaign or battle, but, without waiting for instructions, to march to the thunder of cannon, and render prompt assistance wherever it might be required. It was long before the system was cordially accepted, even in Germany itself; and it has been fiercely criticized.

> To soldiers whose one idea of command might be summarized in the sentence, "I order; you obey," and in whose eyes unqualified and unthinking obedience was the first of virtues, the new teaching appeared subversive of all discipline and authority. If, they said, subordinates are to judge for themselves whether an order is to be executed or not; if they are to be encouraged to march, to attack, or to retreat, on their own volition; if, in a word, each of them is to be considered an independent commander, the superior can never be certain, at any given moment, where his troops are or what they are doing, and to maneuver them as a united whole will be out of the question. Was it likely, they asked, that a junior officer left to himself would act as his superior would have directed him to act had he himself been present? Was it not probable that he would hinder rather

than further the general plan; and would not such untrammeled freedom lead to independent ventures, prolific perhaps of personal glory, but absolutely destructive of the harmony of action essential to success? These dangers, however, had been foreseen; and, while they were recognized as real, they were not considered so inevitable as to forbid the encouragement of an unfettered initiative, nor so formidable as to be insurmountable. The first step was to make a clear distinction between "orders" and "instructions." An "order" was to be obeyed, instantly and to the letter. "Instructions" were an expression of the commander's wishes, not to be carried out unless they were manifestly practicable. But "orders" in the technical sense were not to be issued except by an officer actually present with the body of troops concerned, and fully aware of the situation; otherwise "instructions" only would be sent. The second step was to train all officers to arrive at correct decisions, and so to make certain, as far as possible, that subordinates, when left to themselves, would act as their superiors would wish them to do. The third step was to discourage to the utmost the spirit of rash and selfish enterprise.

In commenting upon these principles Henderson states as follows:

The benefit to the state was enormous. It is true that the initiative of subordinates sometimes degenerated into reckless audacity, and critics have dilated on these rare instances with ludicrous persistence, forgetting the hundreds of others where it was exercised to the best purpose, forgetting the spirit of mutual confidence that permeated the whole army, and forgetting, at the same time, the deplorable results of centralization in the armies they overthrew. It is inconceivable that any student of war, comparing the conduct of the German, the French, and the Austrian generals, should retain even the shadow, of a prejudice in favor of blind obedience and limited responsibility.

"To what," asks the ablest commentator on the Franco-German war, "did the Germans owe their uninterrupted triumph? What was the cause of the constant disasters of the French? What new system did the Germans put in practice, and what are the elements of success of which the French were bereft? The system is, so to speak, official and authoritative amongst the Germans. It is the initiative of the subordinate leaders. This quality, which multiplies the strength of an army, the Germans have succeeded in bringing to something near perfection. It is owing to this quality that, in the midst of varying events, the supreme command pursued its uninterrupted career of victory, and succeeded in controlling, almost without a check, the intricate machinery of the most powerful army that the nineteenth century ever produced. In executing the orders of the supreme command, the subordinate leaders not only did over and over again more than was demanded of them, but surpassed the highest expectations of their superiors, notably at Sedan. It often happened that the faults, more or less inevitable, of the higher authorities were repaired by their subordinates who thus won for them victories which they had not always deserved. In a word, the Germans were indebted to the subordinate leaders that not a single favorable occasion throughout the whole campaign was allowed to "escape unutilized."

Our Own Method

It is hardly necessary to enter into a description of our present system of command—that is familiar enough to us all. Generally speaking it consists first, of "detailed instructions which attempt to provide for every contingency," and second, where the conditions of the case make it possible, of "general instructions supplemented by long and close personal association." There is of course much that is good in the system. It has produced many achievements of which we are justly proud. As a system, however, it can scarcely be classed with that of Nelson and Moltke; it has never stood the supreme test of a large fleet action against a formidable enemy; and it is safe to say that even our greatest triumphs were accomplished in spite of glaring system faults which most of us will candidly admit. These are unfortunately of the sort, which will count most against us as the size of forces, and consequently the complexity of operations, increase. Some of our faults are summarized below to serve as illustrations, though the list is not exhaustive, and others will occur to the reader:

(a) *The present system breeds and fosters a spirit of hostile criticism towards those in authority.* An atmosphere of this sort has permeated the service for a great many years. All must admit that such a condition is lamentable; not only does it prevent that mutual sympathy and understanding essential to cooperative effort, but it also woefully undermines discipline—the primary requisite of military efficiency. So keenly does the writer deplore this most unfortunate tendency towards adverse criticism, that he is loathed to go further in the dissection of our own system. On the other hand a frank examination of existing conditions, with free-minded though friendly admission of defects, is a very healthful process; and it will be doubly justified if by such means corrective measures can be evolved which will eliminate this intolerable evil.

By some the condition of an unfriendly attitude in our service towards authority has been attributed to the American viewpoint and temperament; but, inasmuch as it is known to exist in like degree in some foreign services similarly administered, this explanation is untenable. Hardly more than a superficial analysis of our system is necessary to discover more reasonable causes. Some of them follow: (1) The reasons which govern the actions of seniors are often needlessly kept secret. (2) Juniors lack proper elementary military instruction and fail to truly appreciate the military necessity for unqualified support of, and loyalty to, authority. (3) There is lacking that mutual confidence which is born of common doctrines and of practiced coordination of effort. (4) The task of each person is not always clearly defined nor restricted to its proper area. When a junior is interfered with while executing work properly assignable to him, hostile criticism of his seniors is a natural consequence. Whenever a senior neglects work within his proper province for the sake of giving greater personal attention to duties intended for his subordinates, unfriendly criticism is inevitable. (5) The occasional too rigid enforcement of the letter of regulations. [Spencer] Wilkinson says, "in a narrower sense discipline is maintained by routine. There is a code of regulations to which all must conform. The danger is that weak persons in authority are apt to confuse the form with the substance, and to take the modern conditions, the better organized code of regulations, for the essence of discipline, mistaking the means for the end and the letter for the spirit. A man devoid of judgment may so misuse lawful authority, that without violating the letter of a military code, he may arouse the spirit of disobedience among his subordinates. Discipline is then at war with itself and the results are disastrous."

The spirit of hostile criticism creates scattering of effort, lost motion, working at cross-purpose, and a generally discordant condition; it is indispensable that it be eradicated from the service before effective coordination can be attained. "*E pluribus Unum*" seems lost to the nautical understanding; forgotten in the realm of Neptune. No plan can succeed well without a spirit of loyalty among the several executive elements. Military efficiency cannot be maintained without true discipline, which is only an empty form unless the spirit of the service breathes common understanding, intelligent obedience, and loyalty to authority.

(b) *Only in exceptional cases do young officers get sufficient training in initiative and responsibility to fit them for the higher positions which they are destined to fill in later life.*

The prize essayist of 1909, Lieutenant [Ernest J.] King, says:

> Responsibility and the accompanying exercise of authority, ability, and judgment are indispensable factors in the education of an officer; our officers have too little opportunity in this direction while in the lower grades. They command their divisions only at certain times and under certain circumstances, in most of which they are expected to adhere to certain dispositions already made for them. At present the only opportunity afforded officers commanding gun-divisions to show their ability is at target practice, and even this is an innovation of recent date. Lack of responsibility and the accompanying opportunities to exercise authority, ability, and judgment have often been cited as reasons for attaining command (of ship) rank at an earlier age than obtains in our service. Certainly officers should attain the rank necessary to command ships at an earlier age; but, certainly also, an officer's career should be such that the requirements of the command of a ship should differ from the requirements of the command of a division in degree only. At present our system, if system it can be called, does not call for these requirements to the proper degree while an officer is in the lower grades; i.e., in command of a division.

Entirely apart from their proficiency in other respects, a group of officers, whether divisional officers in a ship or, especially, commanding officers of ships in a fleet, cannot efficiently coordinate their efforts in battle unless each individual possesses the power to quickly and automatically assume initiative and responsibility. Unfortunately the human brain does not respond automatically to any sudden situation unless it has been prepared by training to do so. Proper response is particularly difficult while the individual is under any unusual mental agitation, such as that prevalent in action. [Edoard] Daudignac says:

> "The psycho-physiological disturbances produced . . . in the presence of danger . . . are habitually expressed under the form of collapse or under the form of agitation." There is produced:
>
> (1) Enervation of the will muscles, trembling, arrest in movements, which thereby become disordered and feverish.
> (2) Checked respiration, oppression and restriction of the throat, from which result involuntary vibrations; man is no longer master of his organization.

(3) There is spasmodic contraction of the vessels, paleness, afflux of blood to the heart, dilation of pupils, etc. What is the result? The irrigation of the cerebral cells being modified, man is affected in his intellectual faculties, association of ideas is interrupted, and power of judgment and attention diminished.

[Wilhelm] Balck says:

Our modern personnel has become much more susceptible to the impressions of battle. The steadily improving standards of living tend to increase the instinct of self-preservation and to diminish the spirit of self-sacrifice. . . . The fast manner of living at the present day undermines the nervous system. . . . in addition the nerve-racking impressions on the battlefield are much greater at present than in the past.

The nerves will probably be more severely taxed by terrifying impressions in a sea fight than on shore, and, while this may be somewhat compensated for by greater isolation whereby a smaller proportion of the force will be affected, it must be borne in mind that as a rule only one big fight will occur afloat and the number of veterans will therefore be very small.

Under these conditions the most vigorous possible peace preparation of the automatic functions of the brain is positively indispensable. Otherwise there cannot be even limited assurance that responsible subordinates may be depended upon in battle to think quickly and clearly, to make proper decisions, and to take that initiative and assume that responsibility which is so necessary to effective combination. Preparation of this sort can be a product only of long training [Spencer Wilkinson observed]; a process of cramming is futile; its potent quality is judgment under pressure, which cannot be acquired except through frequent "obligation to decide important practical issues, coupled with the certainty of being called to account for failure."

The necessity for this kind of mental training being admitted, it remains to emphasize the importance of beginning the same during youth and continuing it systematically throughout an officer's career.

It is a fact generally accepted by authorities on the psychology of mind that for the average person above the age of about fifty years, newly acquired knowledge is not readily assimilated; that it does not become an unconscious part of the brain, but remains alien, is obviously "grafted" upon it, and is not subject to automatic use as is knowledge acquired at an earlier age. This age also marks about the turning point in a man's ability to adapt himself to new habits of thought or mental processes, and this ability varies inversely with age. These facts, while indisputable, have frequently been frowned upon because of their assumed implication of a reflection upon older officers; such, however, is far from being true. A properly trained older officer—by which is meant one whose mind is "grooved" to initiative, responsibility and other command qualities—is much better material (even ignoring his superior experience, judgment, and professional attainments) with which to effect combination, than is a properly trained young officer. One "cannot teach an old dog new tricks"; the grooves in the brain of the older man are deep, and will control better in the face of difficulties than will the more shallow furrows of the younger man. On the other hand older officers who have not had proper early training will ordinarily prove less capable in emergency than the untrained youngster, because the mind of the latter is the more pliable and can more readily adapt itself to the unexpected condition.

[David G.] Farragut said:

As a general rule, persons who come into authority late in life shrink from responsibility and often break down under its weight.

This great man was over sixty when his most brilliant work was done, involving initiative and responsibility of the highest order. But his record shows how well he had been prepared for it—how well his mind had been grooved to it. He came into command at the ages of 12, 18, 22, 33, 37, 41, 46, and 57. Some of these involved responsibility and authority well beyond his years and rank, and continued through a considerable period of time. Another conspicuous example of a man well trained while young, who exercised high command with marked success at an advanced age, is von Moltke, who was over 70 during the Franco-Prussian War.

As further evidence that age alone is no bar to efficiency in high command we can all recall personal association with officers old in years yet vigorous in the qualities of command. Is it not a fact that nearly all of these had had the fortunate preliminary training as younger men?

As a most important step then towards developing in the navy the "power of combination"—the "driving power"—it is necessary to make individuals efficient in two of the essential elements of combination; initiative and responsibility. One of the greatest faults in our present system is the failure to scientifically and systematically (instead of haphazardly) develop these two qualities in officers at the time of life when such training is effective in molding the individual. Because in the present generation command rank is not reached until middle age, is not sufficient reason for failing to develop in the younger officers the essential qualities of command; on the contrary it is the strongest of reasons for so doing.

(c) *There is no well-defined doctrine of command—no codified set of rules governing the relations between seniors and juniors.* Personal acquaintance in the official sense furnishes the only safe guide by which a junior may now guess how much initiative is expected of him; and when he may and when he must not depart from the letter of instructions. The same limitation (personal acquaintance) is imposed on a senior in his assumptions concerning the manner in which his orders will be executed. Ordinarily neither senior nor junior can know just where the dividing line is between their two functions; that is, of the co-relative matters not specially mentioned in the orders, what share will be assumed by each, and what reliance can be placed on the other for attending to the remainder. In view of the fact that at present the natural differences due to personality are in no effective manner leveled by application of common administrative principles, as should obviously be done, almost every change in seniors involves more or less radical changes in administrative methods and in the principles of command. In extreme cases these principles have changed from day to day even when no change of personnel has occurred.

Probably every ship in the service is organized and administered differently, depending upon the personalities of their respective commanding and executive officers. Recent cases are known where it was the custom for the commanding officer to personally supervise and direct the most minute details of such work as the painting and cleaning of the ship, and to personally direct the officers of the deck during a great part of the day in nearly every matter that might arise, great or trivial. Contemporaneously in the same fleet the first lieutenants of other ships were allowed exclusive charge of the painting and cleaning and the divisional officers were permitted great latitude in carrying on their division work and watch duty. Between these two extremes could be found almost any degree of authorized initiative and responsibility for juniors in every branch of their work.

The above are differences, not of details, but of principles, and the fact that they exist to-day in our fleets furnishes a great argument for the introduction into the service of a uniform system of command. Under present conditions it is almost impossible for a young officer to formulate in his mind, as the result of his experience, a consistent, logical system for his own guidance in the daily performance of his duties. As soon as one is perhaps fairly started, a change of seniors occurs and a complete upheaval is very apt to follow. This process has been going on for years. What confusion of ideas may we then reasonably expect in the minds of officers of all ranks on the subjects of administration and command?

It requires but very simple analysis to understand that coordination cannot exist without common doctrines, not alone of command, but of administration, of strategy, and of tactics, as well—we must have a common denominator, must speak the same language, or else confusion in the *combined* obedience to an order will surely follow. Such confusion occurs now almost daily in the fleets about the simplest matters; how much greater then must we expect the confusion to be just preceding and during a fleet battle, when even the simplest of general directions can be transmitted only with great difficulty.

It is probable that the proper development of the younger men in the past has not matured partly because of the danger in trusting too blindly to one who may misinterpret the intention of the superior on account of inability to grasp the same viewpoint [paraphrasing Henderson in the January 1912 edition of the *Edinburgh Review*]:

> Initiative is a double-edged weapon dangerous to trust in the hands of subordinates who are liable to misconceive the mind of the chief and are unable to read a situation as he would read it. The keen sword of initiative has no place in the armory of those who hold the "doctrine of no doctrine."

It is perfectly true that the amount of discretion allowed a subordinate must in some degree depend upon the commander's personal knowledge of him. Even [Otto F. W.] Griepenkerl says:

> In practice the amount of independence allowed a subordinate depends on his personal character; a factor that is wanting in the theoretical solution of problems. Yet even in practice the commander of the whole force is sometimes justified to encroach on the domain of even his most tried and trusted subordinate; for the continuity of the whole, the unity of leadership, and the leader's own views and intentions outweigh all other considerations. The preservation of the independence of the subordinate officer must not be overdone. But hampering him with unnecessary details is a much greater error. You must have very good reasons for interfering with your subordinate's freedom of action.

The Germans can, better than ourselves, afford to inject the personal acquaintance factor as a part of their system. In their service the tenure of high command is long, and in consequence seniors and juniors have an opportunity to become thoroughly acquainted under actual conditions of service. With us, on the other hand, there is grave danger of accepting this factor with too great equanimity. Since the tenure in high command is so short it becomes all the more imperative that our *system* be well based upon thoroughly trained officers who can be relied upon for uniformity of decision and conduct under given conditions.

Rather than be deterred on account of insufficient doctrines from developing the attributes of initiative, responsibility and loyalty, in younger officers, it would seem better practice to develop simultaneously both the attributes and the doctrines, since both are vitally essential to reasonable success in modern war, and particularly indispensable to efficient combination.

(d) *The mass of detail handled by those in high positions unduly restricts their time and attention available for more weighty matters.* The condition is particularly acute and lamentable in matters of administrative routine, where, having become firmly entrenched in every day use as a prominent factor in our systems, it is injected automatically into everything that is undertaken, from the piping down of wash clothes or the transfer of an enlisted man, to the management of a target practice.

The causes of the condition are numerous and in part obscure; some of them are summarized below:

(1) Custom and regulations combine to sap the time and energies of those in authority by demanding their attention specifically to many trivialities. (2) The tendency is persistent to hold the top man responsible for the most minute detail without specifically authorizing him to delegate insignificant authority and responsibility. (3) The ship organization as a rule fails to fix clearly the duties and responsibilities of each officer and petty officer. The machine, therefore, requires constant supervision, since the properly subsidiary work of maintenance and operation is in no sense automatic. (4) There is a failure to authorize or to recognize a clear cut "province," or "area of discretion" of subordinates; and a human tendency always for seniors to meddle in the routine work of juniors, due partly to greater familiarity with the work of the latter than with their own.

When one stops to consider the question, it is of course obvious that if the head of a large organization attempts the personal direction and supervision of too many details, his own true work or mission must suffer; and in addition, when an unusually strenuous test is demanded of the organization, such as that imposed on a fleet by war, the power of combination is seriously impaired by a habit, acquired previously, of the important leaders looking ever downwards instead of upwards. Griepenkerl says:

> The commander attends to very few details, as above all things he must endeavor to retain a general supervision over his whole force. Should he attempt to arrange too many details, or interfere everywhere with orders, he would dissipate his energies and lose the power of supervision . . . there is nothing to be gained by such personal interference of subordinates, as he would be assuming duties intended for his subordinates while his own, for which he needs his individual attention and bodily strength, only too easily would suffer from neglect.

And again, commenting upon an engagement:

> The temptation will be very great for General A—to interfere with the main attack by sending it orders, because he would like to see it handled as he himself would handle it were he in immediate command; but such interference would be a great mistake, except it be absolutely necessary, as it might run counter to the plans of the subordinate commanders and fatal disorder would be the result.

Coordinated effort requires fundamentally; first, a division of the work into tasks, each suited to the office, the capability and the capacity of the individual to whom it is assigned; second, a degree of independence for each individual in the performance of his allotted task, duly recognized and respected by those higher in authority; and third (not pertinent to the fault under discussion but inserted to complete the trio of fundamentals), complete loyalty of the subordinate to the general plan of the commander.

(e) *Undue effort and prominence is given to administration.* The ordinary every day duties of administration have grown to be so exacting and to be considered so imperative, that the execution of any special task is accompanied by undue internal friction. Those in authority are snowed under with administrative details (the combined result, as previously pointed out, of regulations, custom and their own volition); and, being thus primarily occupied, little time can be spared for the special task of the day, or for professional study, an essential preparation for war.

Certainly, administration (maintenance and internal operation) is an important function, not only in peace but also in war, but certainly also its importance is subordinate to other functions. Preoccupation in it should not blind us to the fact that by means of scientific organization and high morale, upon which administration is based, its burdens can be very greatly lessened, nor to the fact that administration is but a means to an end and not the end itself. In peace it furnishes a basis for carrying on the special task, and in war it is the machinery of strategy and tactics. If too much time is given to it during peace, at the expense of the special task, the habit will survive during war, regardless of sincere efforts that will probably be made at that late day to reform. This is perhaps the best reason why we should organize and manage our affairs during peace so that those routine and administrative matters, which during war must necessarily be carried on coincidently with the more serious business, should run smoothly, automatically and without the attention of those occupying high military positions.

Unless this be done now, while there is time to stamp it indelibly as a part of our system, we shall find that during war our leaders will each have a task exceeding practicable dimensions, and, together with other important elements, the power of combination will suffer.

Spencer Wilkinson [suggests in *Brain of the Navy* that]

> the two functions of directing the movements so as to secure victories, and of managing the great business concern, have little in common . . . it is easy to see that the chief department of any fighting organization must be that which designs and directs the fight . . . (in Prussia) the distinction was steadily kept in view between the all-important conduct of the operations against an enemy, and the subordinate though necessary business of administration.

(f) *The system of highly centralized authority renders it necessary to issue lengthy orders covering a great number of details.* These are not only very difficult to prepare with even approximate perfection, but they are very difficult for the recipient to digest and execute in the manner desired by the issuing authority. Last winter in the Atlantic Fleet, for example, it was necessary to issue thirteen pages of single spaced typewriting to carry out three simple battle exercises. The number and length of orders and instructions covering a multitude of subjects great and small, issued by high authority, has grown to tremendous proportions, until it unduly taxes the time of all officers to read over the orders issued, and to keep themselves and their subordinates informed with respect to the contents of the same.

Coordination will manifestly be made difficult, in the heat of war, by a personnel habituated to operate only through the medium of excessively long and detailed orders. The pressure of conflict will force the substitution of short, concise general instructions, which in combined operations will surely produce serious confusion, unless their execution is undertaken by subordinate commanders trained to the method and possessing common doctrine of every variety. How often will the failure to execute an important detail be excused by a statement similar to the following: "it should have been done, the necessity for it was obvious, but I had no orders to do so," or the failure to complete some overlooked or unforeseen but essential link in the chain by "my orders were to do so and so, and I had no authority to depart from them."

[Colmer] von der Goltz [observed in *Nation in Arms*]:

> The spirit of the initiative urges to independent action. It renders armies strong. We rightly adhere to the principle that, in the case of an officer who has been guilty of neglect, an excuse to the effect that he had received no orders is of no avail. Passive obedience is not enough for us, not even the mere fulfillment of what has been enjoined, when the occasion has demanded that more should have been done.

Lengthy, detailed orders kill initiative, and engender a spirit of blind obedience to the same to the letter. This is necessarily fatal to combined action because the great objectives are obscured by the mass of detail, and, when the unexpected happens which has not been provided for in the orders (as invariably occurs), the subordinate is not clear as to his mission and is not prepared to further the spirit of the general plan of his commander. Frequently he is deterred from taking any action, without specific subsequent instructions, for fear of actually harming the execution of the general plan.

The German Field Service Regulation requires an order to contain all that a subordinate must know to enable him to act on his own authority for the attainment of the plan of the commander, and no more. Von Moltke's order to move 200,000 men into the field of Gravelotte could be typewritten double spaced on one page. It contained 120 words.

(g) *Until given command it is not known what qualifications an officer has for the same.* There being no systematic training in initiative and responsibility, an officer's first training in these command qualities are frequently coincident with his assignment to an important and responsible post. In consequence it can rarely be foretold with accuracy what efficiency will be shown by a young commander confronted with his first serious responsibility. Many who give promise of being able commanders fail under this crucial test. A system which, from the beginning of an officer's career, forces the development of the indispensable qualities of command, would not only furnish a formidable driving power in all combined undertakings, but would also eliminate to a great degree the uncertainty now existent regarding the fitness of officers for responsible command before their appointment to the same. Instead of such commands being used as a school for the training of commanders, they would become the instrument through which the energies of efficient men could be devoted towards creating and maintaining a higher efficiency than is now known.

A Remedy

In the modern industrial world reformation and development of system are accomplished through four distinct processes, which, according to the authorities in this so-called "scientific management," are applicable in principle to all forms of human activity; they are: 1. A critical examination of existing conditions by experts; 2. Specific recommendation by said experts of a comprehensive plan for betterment; 3. An accurate and detailed recording of results obtained in the practical working of the new plan; and 4. A periodic analysis of the results obtained, with a view to further improvement.

While disclaiming emphatically any intention to pose as an expert on the subject, the writer has in the foregoing paper attempted partially the first step of reformation; that is, critical examination of existing conditions. In order to furnish a satisfactory basis of reasoning and comparison, this has been preceded by an examination of the parallel systems of a few of the great military leaders. He is inclined to rest the case here and omit the second step: that of a specific recommendation of a comprehensive plan for betterment. This, not from lack of positive beliefs on the subject, but because the defects in the existing conditions will in such manner be better emphasized, and because any discussion that may be stimulated by this essay will not fail to recognize the existence of the evils stated. Remedies are at best but tentative, yet the weight of criticism frequently falls upon them, thus obscuring the main point at issue. It is reserved for genius to draw up perfect plans for future guidance. The best that the rest of us can do is to propose something which will serve as a temporary basis for action, specifically and frankly subject to such revision as experience may make desirable in the collective opinion of the service at large; which after all is a good substitute for genius.

The writer would prefer to limit remedial measures to recommending the appointment of a board of experts, in accordance with the best industrial practice, to take the subject under exhaustive consideration. But, for the sake of completeness, and also on account of the strong and well-founded service prejudice against purely "destructive criticism," of which misdemeanor he prefers not to be guilty, the following outline of corrective measures is submitted, with considerable diffidence, and with the reservation that it be considered mainly illustrative, and at best as a basis upon which a tentative beginning may be made.

A. That the [Navy] Department announce as its policy, that, three months after the publication of the order on the subject, the doctrine of the "initiative of the subordinate" shall govern the relations between seniors and juniors. That this doctrine be defined in general orders as follows:

RULE I

All forces shall be organized into groups, each subdivided into minor groups, for tactical and administrative purposes. These shall be:

> Fleets (tactical and administrative).
> Squadrons (tactical and administrative).
> Divisions (tactical only).
> Ships, tactical and administrative.
> Ship Departments.
> Ship Divisions.
> Squads.

Every group shall have a commander whose duties and responsibilities shall be clearly defined and understood.

Normally the commander of any group shall deal only with the group commanders next above and next below him in the organization.

RULE II

"Orders" will be differentiated from "Instructions" as follows:

(a) An "order" is to be obeyed, immediately and to the letter, but will not be issued except by an officer actually present and fully aware of the situation.

(b) "Instructions" express in general terms only, the commander's wishes or "will" and will be carried out only when manifestly practicable. They acquaint a subordinate with his mission, and he is responsible for the detailed manner of their execution as well as for the results of his work as weighed against the difficulties encountered.

RULE III

In the detailed execution of instructions, subordinates are required to restrict themselves rigidly to the general plan expressed by their superior. Subordinates will not ordinarily be interfered with in the detailed execution of their instructions unless it becomes necessary to do so to prevent injury to life or limb, or material injury to property; or unless the successful issue of important affairs would otherwise be jeopardized. Criticism should be reserved until after the completion of assigned duty.

The maximum amount of discretion consistent with success and reason will be given to subordinates on all occasions. These rules are not intended to reduce any authority now existing; but to facilitate the accomplishment of important work and to extend and improve means for executing the will of those in authority.

RULE IV

Seniors will exercise patience and forbearance with juniors during the latter's execution of instructions, with a view to their development through experience rather than precept.

RULE V

Seniors will exercise leniency towards juniors when it is apparent that mistakes have been made only through inexperience and not on account of carelessness or lack of proper effort. Particular leniency is desirable when mistakes occur through overzealousness and where the aim, in spite of bad execution, may be commendable or well judged.

RULE VI

Moderate praise should never be omitted when merited. It is the clear duty of seniors to give censure whenever the same is deserved. Effort should be made to have it understood that all censure is purely impersonal.

B. That between the date of the receipt of the order and that set for it to become effective, all officers be required to read and report in writing that they understand the following:

[George] Henderson—*Science of War* (Chapters I and XII)
[Helmuth] von Spohn—*Art of Command*
[Colmer] von der Goltz—*The Nation in Arms*, Sections II and V

C. That (between the above dates) weekly meetings of all officers be held on board every ship and at every naval station, for the purpose of discussing and studying the principles involved and for the collective reading of Griepenkerl's "Letters on Applied Tactics."

D. That the department's order promulgating the doctrine be posted in every cabin, wardroom, and junior officer's mess room for a period of six months after its publication.

E. That examinations for promotion include questions on the principles of command. To be effective in indoctrinating the service such questions should be framed at least in part on the applicatory system, i.e., the system of "cases" or specific problems.

F. That on board every ship in commission one afternoon a week be devoted by officers to the study of war, including tactical and strategic games played under war college conventions,

In suggesting the foregoing remedy it is recognized that:

1. Before a radical departure from custom and regulations can be tolerated, the sanction and authority of the department are necessary.

2. A doctrine of command to be effective must be uniform and very widely diffused throughout the service. For this purpose general departmental orders are necessary if it is to be accomplished without undue delay.

3. Compliance with an order is not intelligent unless the purpose of the superior is understood.

4. The general acceptance of a doctrine cannot be brought about through orders alone, but these must be supplemented by a general study of the principals involved, and by frequent applicatory exercises.

5. "The time is coming when all great things will be done by that type of cooperation in which each man performs the functions for which he is best suited, each man preserves his own individuality and is supreme in his particular function; and each man at the same time loses none of his originality and proper personal initiative, and yet is controlled by and must work harmoniously with many other men.

TWO

Historical Foundations for Adaptation

Knox challenged U.S. Navy professionals to recognize the transcendent character of maritime operations. His mentor, Capt. William S. Sims, further encouraged Knox to challenge the doctrinal norms of the service, pursue a deeper understanding of maritime affairs, and help solidify the professional foundations of the Navy. Sims congratulated Knox for his two prize-winning essays, "Trained Initiative and Unity of Action: The True Bases of Military Efficiency" and "The Great Lesson from Nelson for Today," and pressed Knox to develop the ideas in those essays, which became the basis for his Naval War College thesis. Upon completing the college's "long course" in 1913, Knox submitted his thesis to the U.S. Naval Institute *Proceedings,* and it became the publication's prize-winning essay for 1915 under the title "The Role of Doctrine in Naval Warfare." In many respects, these essays are interconnected, with Knox consistently revisiting similar themes to make his points.

Knox drew heavily from other authors in his works, often using extended block quotations to carry the narrative. Although his early essays lack complete originality and illustrate a somewhat pedestrian style, they successfully sparked discussion within the Navy ranks. The Naval Institute rewarded Knox with monetary prizes for the articles published in 1914 and 1915. Having addressed challenges of naval leadership in his previous essays, Knox turned to the question of doctrine. The Navy had earlier developed doctrinal texts for planning operations, war gaming, and maritime law. In particular, Knox had studied the lecture pamphlets by Capt. Frank Schofield on planning and the analysis of the nexus between strategy and tactics by Capt. William

McCarty Little. Schofield offered a simple procedure for planning complex naval operations, while McCarty Little provided a methodology for evaluating plans through war gaming. Given these works, Knox then framed an essay to offer fresh recommendations to improve upon existing Navy doctrine in 1915.

Knox directly influenced the curriculum offered at the Naval War College, which exposed U.S. Navy professionals to the underlying historical influences on contemporary maritime strategy. He also emphasized the importance for U.S. Army professionals of exploring similar questions at the Army War College in Carlisle, Pennsylvania. Knox further encouraged the selective assignment of Naval War College graduates to the Army War College and vice versa. Through such exchanges, Knox believed, the two colleges would provide sufficiently focused advanced education for American military professionals to recognize key differences between the land and naval services. Graduates, like Knox, understood the rationale for maintaining two distinct war colleges. Later in his career, he strongly criticized efforts to dissolve the Army and Naval colleges and join them under a unified Armed Forces Staff College and National Defense College.

The fundamental environmental differences between land and sea contributed to an underlying bureaucratic competition that characterized doctrinal differences between the War Department and Navy Department during Knox's time. Following the American Civil War, Lt. Col. Emory Upton, USA, helped influence the establishment of the centralized General Staff organization within the War Department. This organization largely mimicked the model found in the German army. Upton also envisioned a war college based on the German model, although his vision failed to materialize before his death. However, Upton inspired Rear Adm. Stephen B. Luce to establish the Naval War College in 1884. In the reoccurring debate questioning the purpose for maintaining separate war colleges and staff schools for the land and sea services, Knox consistently returned to the original visions of Upton and Luce. He ultimately played a key role in preserving the Army War College and Naval War College during the first fifty years of the twentieth century.

From personal experience, Knox recognized the underlying role of technological innovation in examining the differences between the land and sea services. Army commanders usually faced different strategic and tactical conditions than did their sea-going counterparts in the Navy and Marine Corps. As the age of sail faded in an era of steam and steel, Navy warships generally functioned independently as self-contained fortresses without significant involvement from centralized headquarters ashore. Navy warships rarely operated together in a line of battle, leaving warship skippers inexperienced in coordinating fleet operations. Knox recognized this as a basic problem during the American adventure to suppress Mexican insurgents and revolutionary forces during the 1914 Veracruz campaign. American naval forces struggled under an ambiguous command organization, an unclear mission, and serious logistical problems. Worsening the situation on the ground and in the air, Army commanders attempted to exert authority over their Navy and Marine Corps counterparts. Civilians, assuming authority under their National Guard ranks, further amplified the confusion among American forces in Veracruz.

Having learned from their experiences in Mexico and other counterinsurgency operations in Caribbean and Asiatic waters, Navy officials pressed for the development of a strategic headquarters to coordinate global operations from within the Navy Department. Traditionally, the secretary of the navy had held strategic command over Navy operations, which frequently created problems, as civilian officials had the prerogative to overrule ranking Navy professionals. To streamline the process of making decisions, the Navy's aide for operations, Rear Adm. Bradley A. Fiske, wanted to establish a "chief" of naval operations with authority to assume clear command over the global operations of the U.S. Navy. By this time, Knox had completed service with Sims in the Atlantic Fleet and reported for duty in the ONI in Washington.

The following essay served as a key text for Naval War College students following the First World War and for many years thereafter. In the century since Knox published his prize-winning essay on the role of doctrine, the ideas he offered have resonated in debates concerning the future course of the Navy when considered within the twenty-first century context of "joint" doctrine. In the essay, Knox selectively cited examples taken from foreign texts to subtly highlight the differences between land and sea warfare. In this way, he also justified the imperative strategic contributions of the Naval War College in establishing common doctrinal foundations to guide the operations of the American sea services in both peace and war.

THE ROLE OF DOCTRINE IN NAVAL WARFARE

1915

Motto: *Let us learn to think in the same way about fundamental truths.*
Darrieus

The American Navy acknowledges no superior in its ability to steam and to shoot. If nothing else was required of a fleet of ships in naval warfare we might rest securely in the belief that we are as well prepared for war as any possible antagonist. Strange to say, not many years ago this fallacious belief did permeate the service and was based upon the above narrow, unsound and shortsighted assumption.

Within the last few years, however, a fortunate awakening has come about. The navy is comprehending with greater clearness every day, that a fleet is something more than a mere collection of ships; that a bare "ship for ship" superiority over a possible enemy is not a guarantee of victory; that before ships are ready to go into action, no matter how efficient individually, they must be welded into a body, whose various members can be well controlled from a single source and can act collectively as a unit free from embarrassing internal friction; and that the problem of the proper utilization of the abilities to steam and to shoot—that is, the problem of command—is not only less elementary but also much more difficult of solution than any yet undertaken by us.

Command and Doctrine

The importance of good management to any organization is generally recognized and well understood. In the industrial world, the survival of any concern and production by it of adequate returns for the capital invested, are matters which even the man on the street will admit without argument to be very intimately connected with management. The importance of the latter is indicated not only by the almost universal modern tendency to renovate management, and to adopt more effective, systematic and so-called "scientific" methods of supervision and direction, but also by the fact that the beneficial effects of good management are most apparent in "lines" of business where competition is keen and profits not large. While in exceptional cases an industrial firm may prosper in spite of bad management, it is nevertheless true that management is one of the most important, if not indeed the most important, of the factors which comprise industrial organizations.

The necessity for good management in modern business has become universally admitted as axiomatic. But this general recognition unfortunately does not expand to some other forms of human activity, in all of which the principle is equally applicable that efficient planning and direction are essential to great success. From the trivial routine affairs of private individuals to the great critical matters of state, management, good or bad, is a cardinal element in the results produced.

The business of war, either on land or water, is no exception to this rule. On the contrary, the relative importance of management, as compared with the other ingredients of excellence, is probably greater in war than in any other form of endeavor. This truth is readily understood, even by civilians, when it is applied to the administrative management of a large fleet or army. The professional mind, however, will better appreciate that military management properly includes not only the business of administration but also the leadership of forces engaged, or about to engage, in actual hostilities. Of the two, the latter, or more purely military function of command, is more essential to military success and also requires a greater measure of "scientific management."

The superior importance of good leadership over good logistical administration, in so far as a favorable military issue is concerned, is well illustrated in the naval campaign between [André de] Suffren and [Sir Edward] Hughes. The former admiral was most of the time without a base and unable to obtain sufficient supplies. He constantly contended against scurvy, and an almost utter lack of medicines, provisions and materials of all sorts. His crews were greatly overworked and many ships unfit for sea. However great his administrative ability may have been, it was practically eliminated as a factor in the operations by the conditions, which rendered his fleet destitute of the most vital products of administration. Yet Suffren succeeded through the genius of his leadership in winning from an amply provided and well administered fleet that was superior to his own in size and gun power. The armies of the Potomac and of Northern Virginia in our Civil War furnish another example of the point in question. The former had the advantage during most of the war of the splendid organization and administrative system introduced by [General George B.]

McClellan, and had bountiful supplies. Yet during three years of war this army was so poorly led as to be unable to win from its less numerous Southern opponent, which was unquestionably poorly administered and supplied, but well led.

Good leadership or command, as distinguished from administrative management, is then obviously a cardinal requisite to successful military operations. It properly includes not alone the efficiency of the person in chief command, but also that of the chain of subordinate commanders, which theoretically connects the mind of the chief to each individual in the fleet or army. Command implies control and direction by a leader; but before this is possible with a large number of units, they must be divided into groups, each under the command of a subordinate leader. Each group may be again similarly subdivided and commanded, and if the force be large it may be necessary to repeat the process of subdivision many times. By means of such a so-called "chain of command" it becomes possible to carry into execution the will of the highest leader in a manner, which could not otherwise be done, and to ensure that the entire organization acts coordinately and harmoniously as a unit.

Organization, however, cannot alone produce unity of action in accordance with the desires of the chief. It merely furnishes the mechanism for transmitting, interpreting, directing and executing instructions. It is little more than a bony skeleton, which, though it be an essential part of the organism, must nevertheless be augmented by flesh and sinew and infused with spirit before it can successfully accomplish its mission of life-like coordinated activity conformable to the will of the directing mind.

Moreover, in a military organization it is not sufficient that the "officer-body," which forms the chain of command, shall merely transmit, interpret and execute the orders which are received. They must, in war, frequently act on their own initiative in anticipation of the desires of higher authority. From the very nature of extensive military operations, whether they be afloat or ashore, the commander of the whole force cannot possibly have cognizance of events immediately upon their occurrence. His vision is too limited and his communication system too precarious and slow. Therefore, should he attempt specific personal direction to meet every contingency as it arises, his attacks will be too late to take full advantage of favorable situations presented, and his parries dangerously tardy. Unfortunately in warfare, and more especially in naval warfare, nearly all of the important situations which confront subordinate commanders are of the type which do not admit of delayed decisions. Many of them arise far distant from the commander-in-chief, or occur under other circumstances, such as tactical combat, which make it impossible to defer decision and action while the highest authority is being informed and until his instructions have been received in reply. The time factor is so very pressing and acute in naval operations, particularly in naval battle, that it is normally imperative for the subordinate commander himself to decide and to act, even before his superior can be acquainted with the special situation which has been met. The classic example of Nelson's initiative at the Battle of St. Vincent is far from being the only illustration in history of the necessity for independent action by subordinates in order that advantage may be taken of local situations to assist the efforts of the whole force. Almost every large naval battle ever fought abounds in incidents which illustrate, either negatively or affirmatively, the tremendous importance of such measures being taken by subordinate commanders. The most recent example is the failure of the commander of the Russian second division at Tsushima to form column on the first division at a time when such maneuver was manifestly necessary to avoid a disadvantageous tactical situation. On account of difficulties with signaling, [Zinovy Petrovich] Rodjesvensky was prevented from directing this maneuver.

Of course, in advance of any major operations, the commander-in-chief will usually issue general instructions intended to govern situations that can be anticipated. But the futility of depending upon such instructions, unless they be supplemented by many other things, is thoroughly understood by every officer of experience and every student of history. The possible eventualities are so numerous and complex as to render it difficult in the extreme to foresee many of the critical situations which will arise. Furthermore, when instructions aim to provide against every contingency they are likely to become so comprehensive and voluminous as to be confusing and difficult to remember. Under the stress of hostilities they are frequently forgotten or misinterpreted, and in some cases are deliberately disobeyed either on account of conditions slightly different from those anticipated in the order, or because of conviction of their unsoundness.

The difficult problem connected with the art of command, however, is not how to ensure execution of such wishes of the commander as circumstances permit to be precisely expressed in time to his junior officials. That is relatively simple and easy. Discipline ensures obedience, and the organization provides for the orders being transmitted to the proper places and executed by the forces intended, thus securing due coordination and unity of action, which are always required for the attainment of military success. This problem is one which has been always efficiently solved in our service: our whole system of command is built to satisfy these artificial conditions, with the result that whatever has been undertaken afloat in peace has been well done. Our success during war has also been gratifying, but it should be well marked by such of us who want to make of the navy a real and dependable insurance to our country, that history reveals no occasion upon which a large American fleet has been opposed by a strong, aggressive and numerous foe. It is only in such operations that the true test of our system of command can be made. If, as the author believes, the present system fails to anticipate and to adequately provide for the conditions to be expected during hostilities of such nature, it is obviously imperative that it be modified; wholly regardless of the effect of such change upon administration or upon the outcome of any peace activity whatsoever.

The chief difficulty encountered in the exercise of command is that resulting from a critical situation which imposes upon subordinate commanders the necessity of deciding for themselves the action to be taken, and of carrying their decision into execution, before reference can be made to higher authority. Under these circumstances any system of command is severely tested, and is sure to break down unless it provides adequately for them. If in such cases the decisions and actions of the various subordinate commanders harmonize with the desires of the commander-in-chief—that is, if each one of them does what their chief would do were he present in person—then due coordination is assured and the efforts of the whole command reach their maximum of effectiveness through the resulting unity of action. In other words, the system of command then furnishes a satisfactory basis for the control of the whole force and is adequate to ensure that the will of the supreme commander governs, even in spite of the anomalous condition of its being done in advance on the expression of that will.

It is clear that subordinates cannot be depended upon to comprehend the wishes of the commander-in-chief with respect to situations confronting them, unless they have to guide their decisions something much better than instructions issued before the event and, therefore, necessarily lacking in completeness and applicability. Other measures are indispensable, chief among which is a proper preparation of the minds of the body of officers.

Individually, the officers should be conversant with the theory of war, and familiar with its history and the lessons derivable therefrom. That is to say, education in the art of war, as distinguished from the other numerous branches of the military profession, is a necessary step in the preparation of responsible participants in war. The officers should also be trained in the mental processes which are demanded by active hostile operations. Until the mind receives such training no decision can be in any sense automatic, but must be the result of slow and labored reasoning. Frequently in war, and especially in naval war, it is imperative that decisions be made in advance of reflection, and under the stress of grave responsibility and danger. In such circumstances the functioning of the mind is vastly better if it has been previously prepared by practice in frequent quick decisions involving similar tactical or strategic factors.

In addition, each officer should have previously acquired a spirit of intense loyalty to the plans of his superiors. Loyalty is not merely a moral virtue; it is also a very great military necessity. In the absence of universal loyalty within an organization, the momentous effects which flow from united action are impossible. When loyalty permeates a command its "driving power" is vastly increased, not only because of the greater effect consequent upon cohesive effort but also on account of the stimulating influence upon individual effort.

Besides the preparation which the individual should receive, it is also necessary that the "team mind" should similarly be made ready in advance, before the acts initiated by subordinates can be counted upon to harmonize with the intentions and plans of their common superior. Of course, they should all receive the commander's general instructions and also be acquainted with the plan which such instructions aim to carry out; manifestly, such knowledge is necessary before independent actions can be made to conform thereto. But decidedly something more than last minute preparation of this sort is required. The interpretation of the orders and of the plan by each one of the subordinates should be the same, and so complete and accurate that awkwardness of language, inaccuracies of expression, omission of details or even of generalities, or other defects of the written or verbal instructions, shall not prove a bar to each one knowing the true intentions of his chief, nor to a knowledge of what each and every one of them will think and do under foreseen circumstances or in a sudden and unexpected contingency. Finally, human nature is so constituted that perfect loyalty and cooperation is almost impossible unless the participants are inwardly convinced of the correctness of the plan and methods under which they are mutually acting.

Obviously, then, harmonious and coordinated effort under the pressure of immediateness and during the stress of hostilities, on the part of commanders between whom communications are precarious, is difficult, if not impossible, unless there exists a bond of highly developed mutual understanding and common conviction. The development of such a bond, like the preparation of the individual mind, must necessarily be done during the years of peace preceding war. Of course, mutual understanding and conviction will be accomplished to some degree when the various subordinate commanders are men who have been qualified for their positions by study of the art of war and by training in war games and simulated maneuvers; the loyalty of all to the promulgated plan will also promote common understanding. Yet a much deeper and more comprehensive understanding is required before a band of subordinates can be ready to undertake that kind of coordination demanded by complex and rapidly moving military operations on a large scale. The body of junior commanders must be almost literally of one mind with their commander-in-chief and with each other if frictionless and automatic team-work is to be obtained. Their direction at every point should be unhesitatingly the same as would be given by the commander-in-chief himself were he present. Then, and only then, can the organization fully accomplish its purpose—unity of action in accordance with an expressed plan.

The need for this type of understanding, as well as for the resulting concerted action, should be apparent to anyone giving mature thought to the subject of command. It is recognized as a necessity in the principal foreign military organizations, and they attempt to supply the deficiency through what has been termed "doctrine." Commander [Frank H.] Schofield of our navy has said, "in a military service, where many intellects must cooperate towards a single aim and where the stress of events forbid the actual interchange of ideas, when the need is most felt, there must be a governing idea to which every situation may be referred and from which there may be derived a sound course of action. It is only thus that the full driving power of an organization can make itself felt." Again, in discussing the situation confronting the commander of a fleet on the night preceding a probable battle, the same officer says, "No verbose instructions that he may issue now can have the remotest chance of converting an organization of form into an organization of intellect and spirit. Such a change is a matter of long and patient educational effort that eventually centers around a doctrine of military conduct to which every act either of preparation or of execution is automatically referred. When such a stage of development is achieved a spirit of confidence becomes diffused throughout the service that invests it with a moral power of the greatest value."

For some unaccountable reason the American Navy, and to a somewhat less degree the American Army, have never seriously endeavored to indoctrinate their officers, and thus to furnish a basis for harmonious decisions during hostilities. It is all the more striking that the navy has failed in this respect, because of the supreme importance of the time factor afloat. With us "time is everything," even more than with Nelson, whose conspicuous successes were largely due to the high degree of mutual understanding that existed among his subordinate commanders; and Nelson's indoctrination, more than anything else, made such understanding possible.

Probably all will concur in what has been so far said. It may be summarized briefly as follows:

1. Good management is a cardinal requisite to the success of any organization, industrial or military.

2. Military management comprises both administration and command, of which two the latter is more essential to successful military operations.

3. Command depends not alone upon the orders and acts of the officer directing the entire operations, but also in great measure hinges upon the actions of the chain of subordinate commanders.

4. To properly exercise their command function the officer corps as a body must act unitedly. As a preparation to do this they must be educated in the art of war and trained in its conduct. They must be loyal to their commander-in-chief and his plans, and must possess a deep understanding of the mind of their common chief and of each other.

5. The degree of mutual understanding necessary to unity of action by a large organization, military or naval, can best be assured through previous indoctrination. It is the purpose of this paper to examine into and to discuss the question of doctrine.

Doctrine Defined and Explained

In an unsigned article in the *Edinburgh Review* of April, 1911, the statement is made that "a sound, comprehensive, all-pervading doctrine of war is as important to an army as its organization." This is true to an even greater extent for a navy and it is, therefore, somewhat extraordinary that both the American military services as a whole are unfamiliar even with the meaning of the term "doctrine" when used in its purely military sense, and fail to comprehend its importance as well as its role in bringing about timely and united action in the midst of hostilities.

To many officers, doctrines are synonymous with principles; to others, the word suggests methods; and still others confound it with rules. While all of these are somewhat related none of them may properly be considered as having the same military meaning. The object of military doctrine is to furnish a basis for prompt and harmonious conduct by the subordinate commanders of a large military force, in accordance with the intentions of the commander-in-chief, but without the necessity for referring each decision to superior authority before action is taken. More concisely stated the object is to provide a foundation for mutual understanding between the various commanders during hostile operations.

By recourse to the dictionary it may be learned that doctrine means "whatever is taught; what is held, put forth as true and supported by a teacher, a school, or a sect; it is a general body of instructions; doctrine denotes whatever is recommended as a speculative truth to the belief of others; a doctrine may be true or false, it may be a mere tenet or opinion." One meaning of doctrine is a "principle" or "body of principles," but that is not the sense in which it is employed when applied to the art of war by European military forces. Some military writers and translators have caused great confusion by using the term as a synonym for principles. Military doctrines are beliefs or teachings which have been reasoned from principles; that is, they flow from principles as a source. They are intended to be general guides to the application of mutually accepted principles, and thus furnish a practical basis for coordination under the extremely difficult conditions governing contact between hostile forces.

A principle is a "fundamental truth as a basis of reasoning; the cause, source or origin of anything." Obviously, there is a great difference between a principle and a military doctrine, notwithstanding that they are related. It has been aptly said that the difficulty with fundamental principles lies not in their comprehension but in their application. Under any given circumstances fundamental principles might be correctly applied in a number of materially different ways, depending upon the varieties of doctrines held. Furthermore, in war the number of possible acceptable solutions to a situation is increased not alone by the number of possible applications of the several principles involved, but as well by the variations in the relative importance which may be assumed for each.

One of the best illustrations of the wide differences of doctrine which may be acceptably deduced from the same principles is afforded by the so-called German and French doctrines of war, which at present govern the operations of the respective armies of these two countries. Both doctrines were evolved from exhaustive studies of Napoleonic methods of conducting war, so that both flow not only from the same principles but also from the methods of one man.

Briefly stated the German doctrine of war is that of envelopment. It was argued by their Great General Staff that the power of modern weapons has greatly decreased the vulnerability of the fronts of armies and correspondingly increased the weakness of their flanks. Hence the hostile flanks were chosen as the principal objectives for concentrated attacks. It was deemed preferable that superior numbers be utilized to envelop both flanks of the enemy, while at the same time containing his center. Such procedure necessitated initial deployment by large semi-independent groups over a very wide front, and consequently increased the danger of defeat in detail should the enemy succeed in concentrating on one or more unsupported detachments. To meet this grave danger the several detached parts of the army were each made of such size and character as to be theoretically indestructible, no matter how powerful its immediate opponent, for a time at least long enough to ensure support from adjacent detachments. An army corps of about 40,000 men of all arms was selected as the minimum size of each semi-independent unit.

Due to its wide deployment the control of the whole army by the commander-in-chief was necessarily weakened and rendered precarious, and this fact also seemed to increase the danger of defeat in detail. To overcome this defect the corps commanders, as well as indeed all officers in the German Army, were educated and trained in the same school of thought (indoctrinated), so as to reduce the necessity for greatly centralized command and to always insure unison of thought and cooperative action among separated subordinates under all circumstances. In order to further lessen the danger of defeat in detail, the initiative was to be taken and maintained at all cost. Whenever encountered the enemy was to be vigorously attacked and pressed without awaiting orders, so as to deny him the initiative and also to relieve pressure at points where he may have concentrated. The ultimate aim of the several columns, which started their march on a wide flung front was to concentrate simultaneously on the battlefield itself, marching from different directions and enveloping both flanks of the numerically inferior enemy.

In order that a number of coequal semi-independent corps may avoid defeat in detail during the earlier part of such operations, and may finally concentrate simultaneously and successfully from exterior lines on to the battlefield against an aggressive enemy, it is obviously requisite that great skill and perfect coordination be displayed on the part of the detachment commanders. They must continuously exercise enterprise, boldness, aggressiveness and a high degree of initiative. But above all they must think harmoniously. The actions of each commander must harmonize with those of each of the other coworkers. In reaching any decision its effect upon the operations as a whole must take precedence over the local situation.

In other words, to wage such warfare successfully it is necessarily essential that the subordinate commanders be previously prepared as a team. Manifestly, the work of preparation should be done before the army takes the field—that is, during peace. Nearly all officers must, through study, learn to know war thoroughly from every aspect, and must be trained together as well as it is possible to do by means of sub-caliber games and field maneuvers.

If, during such exercises in common, differences of opinion develop, as will almost invariably happen, personal preference and belief must for the sake of the team success be submerged whenever they conflict with the reasoned and matured conclusions of the majority. Loyal acceptance by all of the teachings of their school of thought is necessary before unity of action can be attained during collective activities. In other words, indoctrination is essential to adequate coordination.

How successful the Germans have been in obtaining the requisite cooperation in spite of the difficulties of so doing which their doctrine of war creates, is attested by the brilliance of their work in 1866 and 1870. True, there were certain exceptions, and at least one prominent general was removed from his command either because of his unwillingness to accept the common doctrine or else his inability to adhere to it. The few exceptions, however, serve chiefly to emphasize with greater force the vital necessity of prescribing doctrine and accomplishing indoctrination, before command of large forces can be successfully exercised. The history of the present war is hardly yet begun and facts are difficult to obtain, but the phenomenal advance of the Germans during the first month of fighting indicates remarkable coordination between the various corps and army commanders.

Attention is here parenthetically called to the essentially similar conditions, as far as command is concerned, between sea warfare and the situations on land created during operations conducted in conformity with the German doctrine of war. In both cases direct control by the commander-in-chief is impossible and his influence is, therefore, liable to crumble. His principal work is of necessity limited to the period of preparation and to the earlier phases of hostile contact. Once action is joined in earnest the commander-in-chief must, both on account of the difficulties of communication and of the time factor, trust the outcome almost wholly to his subordinates; it is then too late for him to materially change the course of events. Hence it soon becomes the function of a number of coequal subordinate commanders to act practically independently, but at the same time to make their respective decisions and acts harmonize with the operations of all the others, while also furthering the plan of the commander-in-chief which has been necessarily expressed in but very general terms. We on the water should particularly heed the fact that this problem in cooperation is not capable of satisfactory solution unless doctrine plays a conspicuous part as one of the favorable factors.

As will be explained later, the French doctrine of war prescribes extreme centralization of command and aims at the control of the whole army by two men supposed to keep constantly in communication with each other and with the various detachment commanders. In operations conforming to this doctrine the situations are comparable to those of a navy operating only during peace, and a study of the French doctrine is, therefore, not so profitable to naval officers seeking the best means for conducting a fleet during war. The principal reason why great centralization is impracticable for hostile operations afloat is not because the various commanders are separated, nor even because communication between them is imperfect, but because of the profound influence of the time factor upon water strategy and especially in water tactics. The exigencies created by the necessity for each situation being met immediately renders centralization fatally weak and makes it of supreme importance that the whole officer corps be indoctrinated in order that it may be capable of synchronous initiative.

The French doctrine of war was developed after the reverses of 1870, and pretends to be a reply to the German doctrine as well as a more accurate interpretation than the latter of Napoleonic war. In the opinion of many profound students the French conception is the sounder for shore work, but is more precarious in that it depends for success upon two men having ability amounting almost to genius; whereas the German doctrines may be put into brilliant effect by men whose intelligence and ability are not necessarily extraordinary.

The French doctrine is based upon application of the principle of the economy of forces. The Germans seek the offensive blindly and vigorously at all points at all times and from exterior lines, whereas the French aim is to husband their troops and to preserve interior lines during a period while the strength and disposition of the enemy is being ascertained. Once the necessary information is obtained however and the time is deemed by the commander-in-chief to be opportune, conservation ceases and the end in view becomes a vigorous attack by almost the whole concentrated army (all the stronger for the interior position and the previous conservation) against the point chosen by the commander-in-chief with the aid of the information which he has awaited. The gathering of the information so necessary to the success of such a grand stroke is entrusted to the commander of a very strong advance guard, composed principally of cavalry and other mobile troops. The task of this officer, and of those under him, is difficult in the extreme. The desired information cannot be obtained without penetrating the enemy's screens, yet an engagement of so serious a nature as to prematurely force the involvement of the entire army must be carefully avoided. The introduction of air craft into warfare has no doubt simplified the task of the advance guard commander, but nevertheless he must be an officer of rare judgment and brilliant attainments. It is necessary that he and the commander-in-chief be exceptionally brilliant men, while other commanders in the army will have few demands made upon their ability beyond that required for the specific execution of orders received.

In the present war it will be remembered that the French left wing retreated continuously from the Belgian border to Paris without once making a decided stand or taking the offensive in force. Probably this was done in accordance with the above described doctrine, their forces being conserved and the interior line being maintained until the commander-in-chief deemed his information sufficiently complete to warrant making a concentrated counter stroke. With heavy reinforcements from Paris the annihilation of the German right wing was attempted with great vigor and apparently came near to succeeding.

Plainly the two doctrines of war described above are directly opposite, notwithstanding the fact that both pretend to be applications of the principles which brought Napoleon his successes, as well as adaptations of his methods to modern conditions. It is probable that studies by other minds of the same master might lead to doctrines differing radically from both the French and the German, yet entirely logical and quite satisfactory as a basis of military operations so long as their entirety was preserved. As already pointed out this probability is due to the differences in the relative values of the several principles involved, likely to be assigned by different students, as well as to individual variations in the manner of applying the various principles to specific conditions.

Any set of men who have read and studied the art of war independently and without collaboration are almost certain to have evolved varying conceptions of war and radically different individual doctrines, each one of which may nevertheless be a sound and reasonable doctrine and bring success if applied collectively by all the subordinate commanders of a military organization. But the reader will readily appreciate the utter confusion and the fatal dispersion of effort that would occur should an army or fleet be commanded by a body of men who have no common meeting ground of doctrine, and who, therefore, must rely separately upon their own differing individual conceptions and doctrines formed by independent thought and reasoning. This hypothetical condition must assume a grave aspect when it is recognized to be the condition of our own navy at the present time.

It should be clear, and well worth mature reflection on the part of our officers, that concerted action by a large force engaged in hostilities requires as its basis common doctrines universally understood and accepted, and that an absence of doctrine is a serious danger to any military force, particularly when opposed, as we are likely to be if opposed at all, by an enemy whose personnel possesses such a bond of mutual understanding.

One is irresistibly led to the conclusion that the formulation and promulgation of doctrine, as well as its acceptance by all concerned, is a practical and an essential element in the peace preparation for war. It is hoped that the foregoing has shown that:

(a) A military doctrine is distinct from a military principle, rule or method, and has an entirely different military function.

(b) Concrete doctrine flows from a conception of war which is based upon a particular alloy of principles.

(c) Concrete doctrine gives birth to harmonized methods, rules and actions.

(d) Universal understanding and acceptance of common doctrines is necessary before concerted action by a large force engaged in hostilities is possible; it is an indispensable element of command, and an essential prelude to great success in war.

Historical Lessons

It would, of course, be too much to say that victory cannot be attained without adequate doctrine, yet this statement is nearer the truth than will be generally conceded. There is little or no exaggeration in the assertions that without doctrine large military operations cannot be carried on satisfactorily against a strong and active foe, and that the influence of doctrine upon victory is profound. Happily, it is not necessary to rely upon argument alone in order to prove the worth of doctrine. History furnishes a number of illustrations from which a good estimate of its value may be made.

Napoleon's first campaign in northern Italy against the Austrians was marvelously well conducted and phenomenally successful. Like the victories of Frederick the Great, these results were accomplished primarily by means of the personal direction of the commander-in-chief at every critical point. On one occasion Napoleon was continuously in the saddle for five consecutive days and nights because of the repeated demand for his presence at various points of the field of operations. Manifestly, that army was not indoctrinated; nor did it require such an aid to coordinate action, because the force was small enough to allow the genius of its commander to be employed in person wherever success was in jeopardy.

While doctrine did not enter as a factor into these early Italian victories, that campaign nevertheless served to indoctrinate in Napoleon's conception and methods of war a number of subordinates. In consequence these men were afterwards able to successfully apply his system during operations of such greater magnitude as to render impracticable the personal supervision of the master at many crucial points.

In the campaigns succeeding his first one, Napoleon handled his army by means of orders assigning a specific task to each of the marshals or corps commanders. Whenever the latter were men who, through plastic intellect trained in Napoleonic methods, had become indoctrinated, the orders almost invariably left to their discretion the manner in which the allotted task was to be performed. In many cases, marshals who commanded practically independent armies operating in conjunction with that under the immediate direction of Napoleon, had very meager instructions, yet were so en rapport with the master as to coordinate splendidly with him. Probably the best examples of this are the operations of Davout and Lannes in the Jena campaign.

The use of doctrine by Napoleon was only one of many elements contributing to a series of incomparable successes, yet it is significant to note that his vanquished opponents relied upon the archaic method of command which was devoid of doctrine and which consequently denied discretion to subordinate leaders.

What value Napoleon himself placed upon unity of thought gained from indoctrination may be culled from his remark after Waterloo to the effect that the reverses of his late career were largely due to the fact that certain marshals "did not understand my system." In speaking of Napoleon's failures of 1813 and 1815 the *Edinburgh Review* of January, 1912, in an article on "The Place of Doctrine in War" has this to say:

> True, he himself, the commander, still knew what he wanted to do, but since his detachment commanders no longer played their part intelligently his army can no longer be considered controllable for the purpose in view and, as a consequence, his mastery over his army was no longer adequate. What is of importance, and of direct bearing on the training and employment of the British Army of today, is to examine the underlying causes of the inadequacy of Napoleon's army in 1813 and 1815 to carry out the master's conceptions. Unquestionably the material of the army had deteriorated, the ranks were full of half-trained conscripts who were not the equal in fighting worth the veterans of the Grand Armeé. Yet when one thinks of how the immature lads of Victor's and Marmont's corps marched 120 miles in four days by one single road through a country almost destitute of supplies, in order to fight at Dresden, one is forced to admit that it was not the men of the French Army so much as the leaders who failed the Emperor. The leaders indeed were the weak link in the chain of command which bound the legs and muskets of the men to the mind of the commander. The story of 1813 and of 1815 is essentially the story of the failure of the marshals. This failure, if analyzed, will be seen to comprise two distinct elements: firstly, a definite want of technical skill in the handling of armies or formations of more than one corps; and, secondly, inability to follow the working of Napoleon's mind, with

consequent failure to understand the method which was the expression in action of his thought.

In this same article it is further pointed out that the disastrous failures of marshals were peculiar to men who had not had the advantage of indoctrination by Napoleon. The burden of war and of government pressed so heavily upon the master's attention that he could not personally attend to the indoctrination of new marshals after old age, wounds, disaffection and death had claimed those who had been of one mind with him. To quote further from the *Edinburgh Review*:

> It is not during the stress and strain of war, when every wheel of the military machine is working at high pressure to grind out concrete results in the shape of movements, operations, battles, that an army can be trained. An army is used in war; it can only be trained in peace; more especially is it only in times of peace that the minds of subordinate commanders can be turned so as to ensure in war the unity of thought and of effort which are essential factors in harmonizing the principles of command.

The prominence given to doctrine in the German system of command has already been spoken of, and the successful manner in which, through its means, the Germans in 1866 and 1870 were enabled to operate large and widely separated forces practically as a unit, is a matter of almost universal knowledge.

In preparing their army for the war with Russia, the Japanese adopted German methods. Needless to say, so essential an element of the German system of command as indoctrination was also included by the army of Japan. At the outbreak of the war the Japanese officers had been educated in the same school of thought and imbued with the same conceptions and doctrines of war. This is equivalent to saying that they thought alike about fundamentals and spoke the same military language. Consequently, misunderstandings of information, reports, or of the intention contained in orders were reduced to a minimum. The various major and minor detachments of the army were enabled to proceed freely with the tasks before them; secure, as each situation developed, in the knowledge of the exact manner in which all the other commanders affected by the same circumstances would act.

With the Russians in Manchuria, on the other hand, it was a very different story. Their officers were not well educated technically and had no such thing as a coherent doctrine known, understood, and acquiesced in by all. Therefore, there was great dispersion and conflict of effort; internal friction was so great as to require most of the energies of the various commanders to over-come it rather than the enemy. In his book on the war General [Aleksey] Kuropatkin often complains of the conflicting beliefs of the subordinate commanders with regard to the training of troops and their employment in the field. He writes:

> Although the same drill books and manuals are used by the whole army, there is considerable variety in the way the tactical instruction is imparted, owing to the diverse views held by the district commanders. . . . Our troops had been instructed, but what they had learned varied according to the personal idiosyncrasies of this or that district commander. The stronger the officer commanding a district, the less did he feel bound to abide by the authorized method of instruction and training laid down in the existing drill books.

In an effort to remedy this condition, Kuropatkin issued comprehensive tactical instructions to his army soon after taking command, and supple-mented these by subsequent instructions. The difficulties of indoctrinating an army or navy faced by an active enemy are obviously great, and a military or naval force so ill prepared as to require such treatment at so late a date is badly handicapped in its endeavors to act as a unit.

That the lack of doctrine was the principal deficiency in the British Army responsible for the severe reverses in South Africa, is a fact which need not be supported here by lengthy discussion. It will be sufficient to state that this opin-ion is held by several eminent authorities, among them General Langlois of the French Army. Probably no more exhaustive study of this war has been made than that by the historical section of the German Great General Staff, which body reaches the same conclusion.

The foregoing illustrations should be sufficient to establish the fact that indoctrination is so essential an element of command that success without it is difficult. But the conservation of the naval mind is such as to forbid the gen-eral acceptance of any new belief or doctrine which is deduced from the his-tory of land warfare alone.

Happily one of the best illustrations of the importance of doctrine to com-mand, and of its use in accomplishing conspicuous success, has been bequeathed by no less a naval genius than Nelson.

The persistent and ceaseless way in which through many years he edu-cated and trained his captains in his own original school of tactical thought is too well known to require more than mention here. He made them almost literally of one mind with himself, so that their acts in the face of the enemy were remarkably harmonious and well-coordinated in spite of an extraordinary small number of signals. At Trafalgar, for example, but four tactical signals were made by the commander-in-chief from daylight until about 4 p.m. In the interregnum, the fleet of thirty-three ships were formed for battle, maneuvered through about six hours of an approach, and then fought an opponent of forty ships for about four hours until decisive victory had been gained. The share that mutual understanding coupled with common convictions (which in effect is doctrine) had in this performance must necessarily have been very great.

The plan given in the famous memorandum of course contributed largely to the mutual understanding as well as to the victory. But it is very essential to the student to note and to comprehend thoroughly that no plan, however well it may be expressed, can possibly be coordinately executed by a large force of vessels of several types operating against a strong and efficient enemy, unless the squadron, division and ship commanders have the same conceptions of war as their commander-in-chief and are well indoctrinated. It cannot be reiterated too often that on the water the element of time will invariably prevent any effective coordination which depends upon signals, radio messages or written instructions. The only satisfactory method of ensuring unity of effort lies in due preparation of the minds of the various commanders, both chief and subordinate, before the outbreak of hostilities. Such preparation comprehends not only adequate tactical and strategic study and training, but also a common meeting ground of beliefs as to the manner of applying principles to modern war.

One does not have to seek far in history to find evidence of the employment of doctrine by such successful naval leaders as [Marcus Vipsanius] Agrippa, [André de] Suffren, [Wilhelm von] Tegethoff and Tōgō Heihachirō. No British admiral except Nelson used it to any marked extent. He sustained no defeats and his victories were conspicuously decisive, while the fights of his kindred admirals never resulted in better than the gaining of a slight advantage.

Moreover, history shows that the badly vanquished fleets have been invariably almost devoid of doctrine. [Zinovy] Rodjesvensky, [Carlo] Persano, [Pierre] Villeneuve, [François-Paul] Brueys and [Marc] Antony almost wholly neglected this important matter. Suffren suffered four defeats before scoring a success. The principal change that took place in his fleet between the first fight and the last one was that only finally did he succeed in appreciably indoctrinating his captains.

The lessons to be derived from the foregoing historical examples, both military and naval, are plainly apparent. The service which neglects so essential a part of the art of war command as the indoctrination of its commissioned personnel is destined to fail in its ambitions for great achievement.

Until very recently the British Army was not indoctrinated and the process is probably not yet satisfactorily completed. Their navy is believed to be behind the army in this respect, which may partially account for some recent disappointments; more especially so when it is remembered that the German Army has been well indoctrinated for forty years and that the Germans are not the kind of people likely to omit so well tried and fundamental an element of command from their sea fighting organization. The Japanese Army is patterned after that of Germany and is indoctrinated; that they have incorporated the same feature in their navy is probable. The advantages of indoctrination has been recognized for a number of years by the foremost French naval students and writers; that their opinions have borne fruit is more than likely. Of all the great navies, our own is probably alone, in completely ignoring this great aid to the waging of decisive war on the sea.

Methods of Developing Doctrine

Within the last two years efforts have been made in our fleet to develop minor tactical doctrine for certain forms of operations. The method used was to crystallize opinion by discussion in conference, of maneuvers held with ships or on the maneuver board, and to adopt the general terms of the consensus of opinion as the governing doctrine. Once determined in this manner the doctrine was promulgated in official written form as the prescribed future general guide to conduct under circumstances similar to those in which experience had been gained by maneuvers. In this way a basis for mutual understanding was progressively evolved which had been reached by utilizing general rather than individual experience and opinion; and which represented the convictions of the majority and the concurrence of all.

Such procedure naturally resulted in the enthusiastic interest of all in the maneuvers, with a consequent gain in tactical development, and was found also to greatly facilitate coordination between ships and divisions on many occasions when communication between them was impossible. Incidentally also, but of great importance, the existence of the doctrine made it possible to simplify and reduce in length the initial and subsequent orders necessary to be issued to carry on the operations. For example, on one occasion, with the doctrine in force, a night maneuver involving the cooperation of about 20 ships and extending over a period of about six hours, was executed exceedingly well in spite of the fact that before the maneuver began the captains were given no information, and no instructions were issued by the commander of the force at any time beyond those contained in a radio order of 44 words sent out at the commencement of the exercise. During the preceding year, practically the same force had performed an almost identical maneuver. In that case, when operating without the advantage of the doctrine, complete information and orders were necessarily issued several days in advance to ensure due understanding by all of the task to be accomplished and to provide for proper coordination during the execution of the maneuver. The orders on this occasion contained over 1200 words and were accompanied by two blueprints showing the track to be followed by each vessel of the force.

While the practical work outlined above has been valuable, and has demonstrated more convincingly than any amount of theory could do the extreme importance of doctrine towards the effective cooperation of vessels acting jointly under conditions to be expected during hostilities, its scope is obviously too limited to be considered as a comprehensive indoctrination of war.

It is manifestly desirable that doctrine should not be built up, from the little things to the larger ones, separately in each branch of the profession as we have done in gunnery and as indicated above to a tentative and minute extent in elementary tactics; but that if effort in all branches is to synchronize, the start should be made at the top. The big questions of policy should first be settled as well as those of command, strategy, tactics, logistics and materiel. Then from such basic decisions minor doctrines may be reasoned to flow logically and consistently so that all parts of the grand scheme will be consistent and harmonious.

In all modern armies manuals are issued for the guidance of officers in the peace training of the men. In addition instructions are issued to govern the general methods and the details of healing the troops in the field. The latter are known as "Field Service Regulations." It is of course intended that these various manuals and instructions shall produce uniformity throughout the army in all essential minor particulars, and, therefore, since they furnish a basis for mutual understanding in the execution of certain principles of secondary importance these manuals may properly be considered as prescribing minor doctrine.

We of the navy are entirely familiar with this form of instruction. For years we have had manuals for guidance in our various lesser activities. We have Infantry and Artillery Drill Regulations, Ship and Gun Drills, The Boat Book, and Gunnery Instructions, as well as The Tactical Signal Book which regulates the interior maneuver of ships in formation. All of these provide for a degree of unity of thought and action along certain lines of smaller consequence.

Yet there is a vital difference between our naval manuals which prescribe minor doctrine and those of the modern army. Ours do not flow from anything higher up, but represent merely a detached work unrelated to other branches of the profession. Almost invariably they are prepared by a board of officers, many of whom have no greater qualification for the task than that of being good all around officers. The product of the board is normally the personal opinion of one or two of its best prepared members, based upon their own study and experience, which is necessarily limited and incomplete. From time to time the manuals are revised, usually by an entirely new board, which inevitably injects its own personal equation into the new instructions. Consequently our manuals are not comprehensive and do not possess the close relationship which is desirable. The revisions do not develop the subjects in an orderly, logical and systematic manner but, due to variable conceptions and doctrines, produce confusion of service thought and practice. This criticism must be tempered when applied to the gunnery manuals, which have been evolved principally from service opinion and therefore do not contain the defects that necessarily creep into the products of haphazard boards. But the tendency to regard the subject of gunnery as detached and more or less unrelated to the employment of the navy as a whole is noticeable even in this excellent manual.

On the other hand, the army manuals of a first-class power are written by the general staff, which prepares itself for the task first by an exhaustive study of history and war, as well as of the material, political and other conditions which confront their country. From the results of this study is evolved a conception of war as it should in its opinion be best conducted. When this broad, comprehensive work of information and that of reflection is completed, and not before then, the general staff having evolved its conception of war formulates its fundamental major doctrines of war, which are made to flow logically from the reasoned conception. So far it is a grand estimate of the situation, with major doctrine representing the grand decisions. From this is sequentially deduced lesser doctrines to be applied in every field of activity. Some of the numerous products are the various manuals and field service regulations which, therefore, fit in perfectly with the grand scheme. The whole is consistent, coherent and cohesive.

Hence it is apparent that to the modern army doctrine is something very real, exceedingly important and decidedly practical. On this side of the water, both ashore and afloat, we are prone to regard doctrine as being evanescent and purely academic—a matter of interest only from a theoretical standpoint. In so doing we eliminate from our services one of the most important elements of military command and a potent aid to victory.

It must not be supposed that the foreign general staffs dogmatically impose their doctrines upon the armies. On the contrary they are careful not to do so, because doctrine which is welded into the organization by the ardent convictions of the body of the personnel is incomparably more effective than that which depends for its support solely upon orders and discipline. Consequently the greatest pains are taken to convert the army to the reasoned beliefs of the general staff. The historical section of the general staff publishes to the service analytical studies of field practice maneuvers and of past campaigns, in which the causes for successes and reverses are carefully explained in such a way as to illustrate and to emphasize the soundness of the doctrines which are advocated, as well as the conceptions of war from which such doctrines have been deduced.

When nations foreign to themselves engage in war, officers are sent from the general staff to observe and record the operations. From the data thus obtained, as well as from other information, the historical section of the staff writes a history of the war and publishes it to the army. Such works are by no means mere records of events, but are profound studies of them. Like the treatment given to maneuvers and previous history, every aspect of the campaign is critically analyzed and the true cause of every important effect is deduced, and arguments are set forth with great care to prove the correctness of the doctrines which pervade their own army. No such accurate, comprehensive and illuminating histories of wars have ever been written than those of the South African and the Manchurian campaigns by the general staffs of the German, French, English and Japanese armies.

In this manner are the convictions of an army strengthened and its morale correspondingly elevated. There is no more important work in time of peace than thus to lay the foundations for united and enthusiastic action after the outbreak of hostilities and for decisive victory as their conclusion.

Concrete Application to Our Own Case

The author has tried to make it clear that the first and most essential step in the process of so indoctrinating a military service as to ensure coordinate action during hostilities, is to improvise and formulate a concrete, comprehensive and coherent conception of modern war.

Napoleonic war was based upon the conception of first shattering the morale and weakening the command of his opponent's army by jeopardizing his communications, and then delivering a concentrated decisive attack in great force at a critical spot in the enemy's line. Moltke's conception, and that of the French following 1870, have been already explained. For the Manchurian campaign, the Japanese adopted the Moltke conception. Nelson's conception of a concentrated attack upon a part of the enemy, followed by a close and decisive action at that point before it could be supported, is too well known to require explanation here. The essential point to be noted is that all brilliant military achievement of modern times with large forces has been preceded by the creation of a conception of war suited to the weapons and conditions of the times, which conception has furnished the basis for indoctrination of the entire force in all branches of activity. That such procedure has been one of the cardinal elements of great success is the opinion of many of the most eminent military authorities of the present day. Similarly, as previously stated, the lack of a comprehensive conception is by many great students considered one of the principal reasons for the failures of the British in South Africa, and of the Russians both ashore and afloat during their war with Japan.

Doubtless the French and Germans have recently brought their shore conceptions up to date. Had either of them failed to do so there might not have been the same equality of advantage as now exists between the two armies, notwithstanding the unprecedented numbers, length of line, power of weapons and other novel conditions presented by the situation.

Whether or not any navy has formulated a conception of modern naval war is unknown to the writer. But in view of the fact that some of them possess general staffs, one of the recognized functions of which is to perform this kind of duty, it is probable that they have not only created the conceptions but have also deduced the doctrines which logically flow therefrom. Consequently it is of great importance that we do likewise if we are to meet any possible enemy as well prepared. The fact that we have no general staff cannot possibly serve as an excuse for neglecting this important matter. The work could probably best be done by a general staff, which fact is one good argument for the creation of such a body; but it is not the purpose of this paper to stray into an appeal for a general staff.

As previously indicated the task of creating a conception of naval war necessarily involves profound and exhaustive study and analysis of naval campaigns, followed by closely reasoned constructive work. In the absence of genius this can be done properly only by a reflective body of officers, qualified from sea experience and professional study, and also by systematic education and training in the methods of war such as may be acquired at our Naval War College.

Once the difficult inductive reasoning necessary to the creation of a conception of war has been done the reflective body can proceed with the easier deductive processes of evolving doctrines out of their basic conception. In the latter work it is imperative that the active fleet be utilized if an objectionable academic taint to the doctrines is to be avoided. The reflective body of officers should cooperate with the commander-in-chief of the active fleet in planning maneuvers, should be embarked in the fleet during their progress and should carefully observe, record and subsequently analyze them. The results so obtained should be used in formulating new or modifying old doctrines, the nature of which is necessarily to some degree tentative and demands that it be acquired progressively. In other words, the creation of doctrine is an evolution.

We of the navy are familiar with the astute manner in which the department has used the collective mind of the service in bringing gunnery up to a high level of efficiency. Competition was introduced to stimulate keen interest which was also further fostered by a system of rewards. In addition the entire personnel was taken into the confidence of the target practice office, thus producing a "team spirit" which engendered the personal enthusiasm of every man and officer afloat in the evolution of gunnery, as well as infused all with a pronounced conviction that we were, as never before, preparing for battle along correct lines.

Some such general method is manifestly necessary before any great progress can be made in the essential higher preparation and training for fleet action and for war in the comprehensive sense.

After the preliminary work has been done by the reflective body, of inductively improvising a grand conception of naval war, from which it might also deduce a few broad general doctrines, the results should be published to the service together with the processes of reasoning which led to the conclusions. This should be presented in such manner as will win the warm conviction and support of most officers. Comment and criticism should be invited and also published.

The carefully planned fleet maneuvers should be put on a competitive basis; otherwise the interest necessary to obtain the best thought of the officers may not be aroused. Most important of all, the maneuvers should be followed by a free discussion in writing and in conferences by all officers above a certain rank, not too low, say lieutenant. Only in this manner can the service be made to feel that the resulting doctrines are born of themselves and not imposed upon them, and such sentiments are absolutely required before the collective mind, which is akin to genius, can efficiently be utilized.

Only by some such general method will it be possible to arrive at definite conclusions concerning the larger questions of the profession. All will agree that the present rather aimless drifting of thought in these matters should come to an end if we are ever to bring the navy to the point of real readiness for major hostile operations. It is true that there is danger in undue rigidity; but while by the method advocated, thought and doctrine will become partially solidified, it will also remain sufficiently plastic and tentative to permit changes which will inevitably be necessary from time to time to keep up to date. Without change, there can be no progress; the acquisition of doctrine is not only a process requiring the utilization of the collective mind of the service, but is also a never-ending progressive one.

To reach the ultimate goal of war efficiency we must begin with principles, conceptions and major doctrines, before we can safely determine minor doctrines, methods and rules. We must build from the foundation upwards and not from the roof downwards.

For example, it is important to determine whether our strategic and tactical operations shall be offensive or defensive in character, and whether they are to be introduced by "secondary warfare" (mines, destroyers and submarines) or by "primary warfare" (the employment of the whole force); whether the fleet will form in ordinary simple column or in an alignment of groups; whether a parallel fight is to be sought or a concentration of superior force at one or more points, and if the latter how and where; whether each type of ship will be concentrated or the whole force divided into groups, each comprising several types; whether we will attempt to fight by exterior or interior lines; whether destroyers are to endeavor to cripple the enemy by a night attack preceding the general engagement or to be used only during the main fleet action; whether submarines shall adopt eccentric plans or be utilized jointly with the rest of the fleet; whether information is to be obtained by wide flung distant scouting or only by close scouting; whether our system of command is to provide the freedom of the initiative to subordinate commanders or will depend upon centralized direction by the commander-in-chief, etc.

The determination of such matters as these produces a "conception" of war which furnishes a point of origin, without which we are as uncertain of our bearings as a vessel in a fog. To leave such questions to the individual choice of succeeding commanders-in-chief invites the present state of chronic indecision and chaotic confusion of thought throughout the service, and debars us from the benefit of permanency in any progress that may be made.

In concluding this paper it is not out of place to call attention to the fact that the need for unity of service thought is not confined to the floating forces. The preparedness for the fleet for war is closely related to the efficiency of the shore establishment, from which its material wants are filled and upon which it depends for the inception and general direction of its active work.

The Navy Department is composed of a number of semi-independent and somewhat loosely organized and coordinated divisions, bureaus, board and offices, all under the charge of a civilian head who is dependent upon them for advice on technical and military questions. With the best and most honest intentions, the departmental advisers must necessarily give conflicting counsel unless they belong to the same school of thought; and when no school of thought exists it is inevitable that nearly every officer should have a somewhat different viewpoint and should often hold an opinion at variance with that of every other officer. Consequently it is to be expected that not infrequently each one of the Secretary's advisers will differ in his recommendations from all of his contemporaries in office, and that rarely can a consensus of opinion on any given question be reached.

The disastrous results that must follow a failure in Washington to hold similar views about fundamentals are apparent. There can be no fixed policies, no enduring organization, no uniformity of rules and methods and no stable progress. Fleet efficiency must become the football of momentary expediency. Things done today will be undone tomorrow and again done the day after. Who is to blame? Surely not the civilians of the government who have long since learned to regard professional advice with suspicion. It is we ourselves who are at fault and we can fairly blame neither Congress, our form of government, the un-military characteristics of the people, nor any civilian official.

There is no complete cure for any bad condition, and it would be foolish to claim that universal concurrence in a school of thought could absolutely eradicate all these evils; but on the other hand, in the opinion of the author, such a remedy would go farther to alleviate the troubles indicated at the seat of government than any other single measure that could be adopted.

Both ashore and afloat we, therefore, imperatively need first of all a conception of war. Once this is created we will be enabled to proceed, with our eyes open and our course well marked, towards a coherent comprehensive scheme of naval life. Doctrine, methods and rules may be made to flow consistently and logically, therefrom. Strategy, tactics, logistics, gunnery, ship design, ship exercises, shore and ship organization and administration—every ramification of the profession—may be developed with confidence and wisdom, and harmoniously interwoven to produce, not merely the present heterogeneous body with a few efficient parts, but exclusively efficient parts well knit into a competent and homogeneous body.

THREE

The Ethos of American Naval Command

The breezy Caribbean winds and sandy beaches of Cuba inspired Knox to study the maritime history of the area. Reporting in 1916 as the commanding officer of the U.S. naval base in Guantanamo Bay, Cuba, Knox guided his wife, Lilly, and son, Dudley Jr., to historic sites on and around the island, sailed to mythologized pirate coves, and reveled in the maritime atmosphere of the Caribbean. Having published the prize-winning essay "The Role of Doctrine in Naval Warfare" one year earlier, Knox received an invitation from Capt. William S. Sims to return to the Naval War College. Then serving as president of the college, Sims wanted to expand the curriculum beyond dogmatic discussions of strategy and tactics. He wished to examine the concept of "influence" in maritime strategy in addressing less tangible factors of human psychology. In correspondence, Sims pressed Knox to accept orders to the Naval War College staff. Concurrently, Sims asked Ernest J. King to join the Naval War College staff. Knox delayed while King declined outright, choosing instead to accept orders with the seagoing staff of Vice Adm. Henry T. Mayo, the commander in chief, Atlantic Fleet (CinCLant).

Knox and King understood the potential influence of the Naval War College upon the future success of the Navy. At the same time, both recognized the importance of securing assignments within the seagoing ranks—preferably in command of a warship or, alternatively, with an admiral who had the influence to arrange command of a warship. In 1916 Knox and King held rank as commanders and shared similar aspirations for promotion to captain. Both understood Sims' vision, but the Naval War College struggled under budgetary challenges, politically charged congressional investigations, and a poor reputation within the seagoing ranks. One contemporary explained the reluctance of seagoing officers to accept orders to the Naval War College:

> It was far from being a place where only officers "going places" in the Navy or "the brains" were detailed by the Bureau of Navigation. The War College was a perfect place to send officers whom the Bureau wished to put in a specific slot the following summer, and needed to be kept on ice for the ensuing year. It also was a perfect place to send an officer for whom, at the moment, the Navy had no appropriate detail. Unfortunately, it also was a place where an officer, whom nobody in command really wanted at the moment, or anytime, could be kept for a year, with the hope that a turn in his health or the ceaseless pruning of the Selection Boards would eliminate him as a detailing problem.[1]

Although the institution suffered from a diminished reputation within the Navy, Sims remained an attentive mentor after Knox and King declined assignments to the Naval War College in 1917.

Sims nurtured the reputation of the Naval War College within the service and in the popular arena. He relied upon personal connections within Congress to circumvent rivals within the ranks of the Navy. With rank as a rear admiral while serving as the Naval War College president, Sims received unexpected orders in 1917. He sailed incognito to London in April, later assuming temporary rank as a three-star admiral with the title of commander, U.S. Navy Forces in Europe, American Expeditionary Force. After the First World War, he lobbied the younger cousin of former president Theodore Roosevelt, then Assistant Secretary of the Navy Franklin D. Roosevelt, to launch a campaign to fundamentally overhaul the command, doctrine, organization, and culture of the Navy. Sims severely criticized Secretary of the Navy Josephus Daniels for failing to prepare the Navy in anticipation of the First World War. The rebellious tone Sims and his associates employed in their quest for reform stirred significant controversy. Roosevelt eventually thought Sims had violated a basic rule in American civil-military traditions, and while he nurtured a fondness for the sea services, he criticized Sims and other Navy officers as being "holier-than-now" and "gold laced gentlemen."[2]

Within the ranks of the Navy, Sims pressed fellow professionals to develop a deeper understanding of global maritime affairs. After returning from the European warfront in 1919, Sims helped organize a board under Knox, with King and Pye to assist, whose task it was to write a manifesto designed to overhaul the Navy. Known as the "Knox-King-Pye board," its recommendations drew significant attention within the Navy and in popular media. It emphasized the crucial strategic failure of the Navy to nurture professionals within the service with an advanced education in the literature of war.[3] The following essay, "The Elements of Leadership," appeared at roughly the same time as the Knox-King-Pye recommendations. The Naval War College president, Sims, made Knox's essay required reading, such that Cdr. Harold R. Stark synthesized the essay as part of a reading guide that circulated among fellow class of 1923 students, including Capt. Thomas C. Hart and Cdr. Chester W. Nimitz. Knox had already weighed in on this discussion in this essay, "The Elements of Leadership," so Knox encouraged King to publish a similar article, which appeared in U.S. Naval Institute *Proceedings* as "A Wrinkle or Two in Handling Men."[4]

Writing in tandem on the challenges of naval leadership, Knox and King influenced Navy concepts of maritime operations through the Second World War and beyond. While their perspectives of naval leadership reflect the times in which they served, our Navy has consistently revisited problems of leadership. In his essay, Knox provided a clear analysis of the challenges of naval leadership and then offered clear recommendations for application within the service. The 2014 edition of the service's Navy Leader Development Strategy addressed similar questions, and the reader will find potential answers within the text of Knox's essay.

THE ELEMENTS OF LEADERSHIP

1920

In its broadest sense Leadership encompasses the entire profession of the officer and is virtually synonymous with officership. But we are not here concerned with those aspects of the subject pertaining to "higher command." In a more restricted, and probably a better technical sense, Leadership relates primarily to the handling of subordinates; which is the paramount function of officers. Even in the multifarious duties connected with material, the officer's primary role is the handling of men who manipulate the material.

The practice of any art is facilitated greatly by knowledge of and skill in related arts. The dentist must know something of medicine and surgery; the seaman and the aviator require familiarity with meteorology, etc. So it is with Leadership. The leader of men is handicapped seriously without a good working knowledge of such arts as organization and administration. This is a necessary foundation for Leadership. Moreover, proficiency in leading men, as in all other forms of human endeavor, is immensely furthered by knowledge of the governing principles. Once principles are mastered, sound practice follows inevitably. Ignorance of principles limits and retards tremendously the development of proficiency; it compels the practical man to grope and flounder; to learn only through laboriously repeated experience, which he can analyze and profit by only with much difficulty and serious waste of time. Principles serve as a compass—a practical means to point the direct course.

For these reasons it is considered that the most practical and helpful method of treating our subject is primarily to formulate principles; and then to give such consideration to their application as time will permit.

Principle I

A LEADER MUST EXERCISE CONTROL OVER HIS SUBORDINATES

This is the basic principle; the need for which is too well understood to require argument. What concerns us here is how to get this control. In the navy, law and regulations provide ample authority for duly constituted leaders. But unless such authority is actually exercised, it is valueless. How often have we seen young officers and petty officers virtually impotent because they knew not how to exercise the authority, which was theirs? Occasionally even old officers are seen who have failed to develop in themselves sufficient capacity for Leadership, and hence are unable to use their authority effectively and to control properly their subordinates.

To a great extent control over men is influenced by the leader's "military character," which will be discussed later. Organization is another important element, more especially as the number of men increases. But the basis of control is discipline. Subordinates must obey if the fundamental purposes of a military organization are to be accomplished.

Punishment is usually associated prominently with discipline. It is more logical to link it with indiscipline. The need for excessive punishment, in degree or frequency, is certain evidence of bad discipline; which can be corrected best, not by punishment as a primary agency, but by good morale established by a type of Leadership in which punishment plays a minor role.

On quiescent occasions the specter of punishment, however sorry a substitute it may be for good morale, may be adequate to obtain satisfactory obedience. But in battle, or other emergency—such as "man overboard," fire, collision, etc.—the mere ability to obtain obedience, through either fear or good will, is not sufficient; at such times of crucial test, obedience must be prompt to an extreme, virtually instinctive, if panic, failure, loss of life, or defeat, [*sic*] are to be averted and success achieved.

Instinctive obedience in crises cannot be obtained without enlisting the aid of habit; because under unusual mental tension the average mind escapes the ordinary rule of the will, and habits alone dictate conduct. However important the function of drills in promoting mechanical efficiency, such effect is of less value than of instilling a habit of obedience. The officer who fails to exploit this aspect of drills; who permits men to obey leisurely, to answer back, to be slovenly in bearing, etc., may possibly accomplish something towards improvement in mechanical manipulation, but the net result will be positively harmful, owing to the promotion of a habit of indiscipline—a habit which will cost lives in emergencies.

The need for instinctive obedience in order to save life and ships, and to win battles, is the great impelling reason for the ceremonies and conventions of military life; and for general "smartness" of every kind. These tend constantly to create a habit of subordination and obedience to proper authority. It may appear to be a stretch of imagination to contend that strict observance of the salute and other minor formalities will play an important part in meeting major emergencies successfully, yet it is a fact; because the habits thus formed by repeated daily observance promote in great measure that control without which disorganization and failure readily occur under stress.

It is said that until the first gas attack the Canadians of all ranks were impatient of and inclined to ridicule these seemingly petty conventions. Their bitter experience then, when a great number of lives were lost unnecessarily through the breakdown of military control, convinced them of the vital importance of tautness in minor military etiquette. Thereafter the Canadians made a fetish of such things and soon became a crack fighting army. The earnestness and thoroughness with which the quickly created American Expeditionary Forces observed the salute and other formalities undoubtedly contributed more than any other single factor in their early readiness for active service, and their excellent showing in battle. There can be little doubt of this fact when we contrast the superb performances of American troops in Europe, with the many disgraceful incidents in American history of which troops were guilty who scorned the apparent trivialities. When the Bolsheviki abolished the salute, the troops left the trenches and sold their artillery. It was only after the fallacy of their theories had been proved that the Bolsheviki resorted to the harshest discipline in Europe, and began to be successful.

The hand salute, the "sir," the cheery "aye, aye," standing at attention, piping the side, parading the guard, gun salutes, etc., are all marks of respect, subordination and courtesy, of the highest utility in promoting control through habit. It is not a trivial duty that every officer shall himself be punctilious in these matters; nor that he should take sufficient pains to keep others up to the mark. In view of the regulations and well-established custom in these conventions, their neglect constitutes an act of indiscipline; which if repeated often will surely lower our cohesion and efficiency in emergencies, through the strong psychological influence of habit. To blink at these things is to train falsely.

On the other hand, there is danger in overdoing etiquette, ceremony and smartness, and of defeating their own ends by reaction. An overdose, psychological or physical, is frequently more harmful than an under dose. It is just as essential not to keep men standing at attention without sufficient reason, as it is to do so when proper occasion demands. Subordinates should not be expected, nor required, to salute when engaged in occupations requiring their concentrated attention; nor under unusual circumstances where its omission does not constitute obvious neglect. Tact and a sense of appropriateness are required. When the occasion calls for etiquette and ceremony, habitual and punctilious smartness should be insisted upon; but when they are out of place, informality and relaxation should be provided for just as carefully. The preservation of this balance is a mark of good officership.

The stabilizing influence of habit facilitates greatly the needful control over men's volition. Discipline, built up by habit, furnishes a strong impulse to obey orders from higher authority, when excitement in any form tends to undermine the mental control, which men normally exert over their individual actions.

Habit serves the purposes of Leadership control in another way also. Occasions will arise when emotion is so strong as almost to eliminate volition and will power, and men's actions will become largely mechanical. Under such conditions habit will dominate their actions; they will automatically revert to the mechanical processes to which they have been habituated previously. For example, a well drilled gun's crew, under a fire so heavy as to upset their mental equilibrium, will continue to serve their gun in a purely mechanical way, much longer than will a gun's crew whose drill has been neglected. The mechanical habits established by conscientious drill may become of vital consequence to control in battle. Habit is then doubly essential as a stabilizer for control. It furthers control through discipline, while volition is active, and also through automatism, when actions become merely mechanical.

But when the emergency is great, or emotion from any cause is at its height (when the gun's crew gets panicky), habit alone cannot be relied upon to ensure adequate control; more especially when it becomes necessary to perform some act to which the organization has not been habituated. Under such circumstances a leader may require not only the emergency brake of habit, but also an accelerator; which will be at his command if he is proficient in the art of suggestion, and understands the elements of crowd psychology. Such knowledge will also be useful as an aid to control under normal circumstances.

Both for individuals and crowds the following conditions favor their responsiveness to suggestion:

(a) Highly concentrated attention on one subject.
(b) Monotony of external surroundings.
(c) Restriction of bodily movement.
(d) Fatigue.
(e) Emotional excitement.

If the suggestion to be made is for immediate action, the most effective manner of making it is by example, more especially the example of a recognized leader of high prestige. Oral persuasion or direction is useful, but not so effective as the example of immediate execution.

When the object is not one calling for the immediate action of the crowd, but is to impregnate their minds with beliefs, other means of suggestion are best utilized. Simple affirmation, free from reasoning is very effective; especially if repeated constantly, monotony of repetition being carefully avoided by interspersing a variety of other related ideas. In addressing a crowd the effect of the last impression given is much greater than any previous ones, and this fact should always be utilized.

Psychology is rapidly emerging from the domain of fakirs and becoming more and more the concern of those practical men whose work requires the handling of other men collectively. In these modern times no leader can be considered proficient until he is able to turn to practical account some of the well proven aspects of psychology.

Besides certain attributes of character in the leaders themselves, and good organization, the principle of control requires first of all good discipline, in attaining which habit is the most valuable aid; second, sufficient drill and training to induce excited men to perform their respective tasks automatically; and third, facility in utilizing the power of suggestion.

While it is essential that leaders shall establish mental supremacy over their men by the above means, in order to control them properly; [*sic*] it is equally necessary that such domination shall not be so prominent as to incur their constant instinctive resistance. It is much better that the control be achieved almost without the subordinates themselves realizing it. This can be made possible only through a condition of psychological harmony; which will itself react in furtherance of control.

Principle II

PSYCHOLOGICAL HARMONY WITHIN AN ORGANIZATION IS INDISPENSABLE TO ITS GENERAL EFFICIENCY

This is the second great principle of Leadership.

Whatever control is enforced over inwardly rebellious men costs undue friction and effort to overcome their hostility; and consequently the efficiency of the work in hand is lessened by the wasted effort involved. But, worse than this, repeated control in spite of covert opposition, forms a pernicious habit of insubordination in those so controlled, which inevitably will prove a serious menace in emergencies.

On the other hand, a condition of psychological harmony is a constant aid to the efficient performance of any task; and whenever such condition is habitual, it furnishes a most valuable means of inculcating instinctive obedience, and of creating the very highest state of discipline and general efficiency.

When we consider the importance of psychological harmony, together with the adverse influences of normal military and naval conditions—such as the surrender of personal freedom, the discomfort, hardship, and danger, and the many other detrimental circumstances familiar to all—it is apparent that this question requires constant attention, and proficient handling, if the officer is to be a successful leader.

(a) ***Justice*** in the exercise of authority is a basic element in psychological harmony. This truth is too well understood to require argument here. It is important to note, however, that what counts most in establishing the spirit of harmony is not the fact of justice prevailing; but a general belief that such prevalence exists. The justice must be obvious to all. Pains must be taken by leaders, without undignified advertising to establish the conviction among their subordinates that impartial justice is a primary consideration in the exercise of authority over them.

(b) *Understanding.*—As a rule the men and younger officers lack conviction as to the genuine need for many of the apparently minor requirements of military and naval life. Without such conviction these things undoubtedly assume an aspect of imposition and sometimes even of persecution; and cheerful compliance with requirements is then impossible. To couple an excuse or an explanation with every order obviously is to weaken authority and control. Yet if men are kept habitually in ignorance of the purpose of their orders, a great incentive to a cheerful spirit is necessarily lost. They must be kept generally informed of events pertaining to their work and of the intentions of those in authority, if the human interest and good will essential to the best accomplishment are to be aroused and maintained.

Of course it is not always expedient immediately to inform subordinates fully of the reasons for orders. But pains should be taken to do so as early as practicable. Meantime it is of the utmost importance that officers refrain from habitual growling and impugning the motives of higher authority. This is a most pernicious practice which promotes serious misunderstanding and a spirit of mutiny.

Information pertaining to current work is not all that is needed. If men are to submit cheerfully and willingly to our somewhat annoying customs and conventions, they must first be convinced that these troublesome usages play an important and necessary role in naval efficiency. The good health of men crowded together on board ship requires scrupulous cleanliness both of person and of habitation. This obvious fact is overlooked by many thoughtless men unless their attention is drawn to it with some frequency; preferably supported by data. Neatness and orderliness are indispensable to coordinated effort; more especially under crowded conditions and in emergencies. Cleanliness and neatness both stimulate self-respect, without which men and efficiency degenerate rapidly. The role of etiquette, form and ceremony of all kinds, in creating and maintaining discipline—the lifesaver in emergencies—is more difficult to make men understand. But the pains needed to explain the underlying reasons for all these matters, so peculiar and inexplicable to the average recruit and even to many others, is more than repaid by the gain in psychological harmony.

Men must understand the objects and reasons for any troublesome effort, if they are to give a whole-hearted response to the demands made upon them.

(c) **Comradeship.**—Probably the most important of all the elements of psychological harmony is a spirit of comradeship. It is the surest antidote to the inevitable enmity felt by men reared in a democracy against what seems to them the despotic leanings of the military services. Strangely enough there has been less comradeship between American officers and men than between those of some European services. During the late war, the principal point emphasized by the British in the training of the large number of new officers was the imperative necessity for their establishing a bond of comradeship between themselves and their men. British practice in this regard perhaps would have a color of paternalism and patronizing that would be objectionable to American men. Nevertheless the principle is sound, and there is every reason why we should apply it; adjusting our methods to suit the conditions confronting us. It is of course very essential to avoid undue intimacy and familiarity, which the men themselves dislike and which experience has shown to be so disastrous to discipline and proper control over men. The requirements of Leadership impose some degree of reserve on the part of seniors and appropriate deference from juniors. When these bounds are overstepped Leadership is undermined; yet if they are too inelastic the consequences are equally detrimental. Good leaders learn and follow a middle course; which is not difficult for officers who have acquired poise, self-possession and *savoir faire*, and who have a fraternal feeling towards their subordinates.

Those who really feel comradeship will give unmistakable evidence of the fact in the numerous ways in which feelings are manifested to others—by bearing, manner, tone, general expression, etc.—ways difficult to define but familiar to all. Officers should strive to foster by their own expression reciprocal feelings towards themselves by the men; and to avoid careless rebuffs to their subordinates, who are apt to be hypersensitive.

An active earnest practical interest in the general welfare of subordinates is essential to feelings of comradeship on their part towards seniors. A good officer will keep an eye on his men's mess, to see that they get good food well served. He will be watchful that excessive work is not required of them without necessary cause; that through accident or design they are not deprived of money, leave and privileges which are their due; that unnecessary discomfort or other aggravating conditions are not imposed upon them; that they are not punished unjustly; that they have adequate opportunity and means for healthful recreation, etc. In these and many other things the officer must exercise foresight and take the initiative to safeguard the general welfare of his subordinates; many of whom through ignorance or diffidence will refrain from making reasonable protests, yet will harbor feelings of dissatisfaction and resentment against annoying circumstances. Furthermore, a good officer will not hold himself too much apart from his subordinates—be they officers or men. Nothing contributes so much to a proper spirit of comradeship as a degree of sociability; more especially when combined with courtesy, cheerfulness and humor. Subordinates should be talked to, frequently, in a friendly human way, and not treated as though they belonged to a different species. A kindly "good morning" with a few words of personal interest goes a long way towards maintaining a spirit of comradeship.

It is also highly important that a directly personal relationship be established with each subordinate. Each one should feel that this individuality is not submerged into the impersonal mass of the organization; but that his own self is a distinct personality in which his seniors have a direct human interest. The daily work will offer ample opportunities for this; but it can be done most effectively whenever men are in trouble, or desire a special favor. A keen personal interest exhibited at such times solidifies the personal relationship in an amazing way. Such a relationship makes it possible to handle successfully those with incorrigible leanings, and to command the good will and comradeship of all, to a degree that is otherwise impossible.

(d) **Recreation.**—A reasonable amount of recreation is normally essential to the mental wellbeing and contentment of men;

especially when they occupy positions of but little responsibility. It is an important part of a leader's function to provide diversion of a form sufficiently interesting to serve as recreation for their subordinates. The peculiar conditions of military and naval life frequently deny men opportunity for ordinary kinds of recreation, and at times unduly attract their attention to pernicious amusement. A good officer will be active and resourceful in devising and providing means for healthful, interesting recreation for his men, and will encourage their participation in it. Some tact is required on his part in guarding against too much paternalism, or too great a color of officialdom, both of which are distasteful to men in matters of recreation. If the means and opportunity are provided at the men's own suggestion, so much the better; but in any event the officer should keep in the background once any particular form of recreation is well started.

Justice in the exercise of authority, *Understanding* by subordinates of the reasons for the requirements and orders of higher authority, a *Spirit of Comradeship* between all ranks and ratings, and adequate *Recreation,* are four primary factors in the principle of psychological harmony. This principle is closely affiliated with that of control, the first one considered. They afford each other mutual support and furnish a good groundwork for Leadership of men. But these are not all of Leadership; otherwise we might be content to command a herd of cows, in which control and psychological harmony are normally developed highly. With organizations of men, idealism or some other kind of inspiration is indispensable, if great achievement is to be counted among their capabilities. This leads us to the third principle.

Principle III

SOME DEGREE OF EMOTIONAL INSPIRATION IS ESSENTIAL TO THE HIGHEST EFFICIENCY

The old prejudice against "too much contentment" has its origin in a belief that marked contentment can exist only as the result of slackness, and therefore of inefficiency. There is some ground for this belief; but only in cases where the officers are deficient in the art of Leadership. With good leaders the most efficient organization is the most contented; a combination accomplished principally through various forms of emotional inspiration, the most important of which will be discussed below.

(a) ***Interest* is a great stimulus to effort and achievement.** When interest flags efficiency necessarily depreciates. When interest is aroused and maintained at high pitch, capacity for work and for accomplishment is greatly enhanced. A common method of killing interest is by unwarranted interference in the province of subordinate officers and petty officers. Both their province and their pride must be respected if their interest is to be sustained. Many ways of exciting and maintaining interest will suggest themselves to the resourceful leader; but most important of all is for him to exhibit repeated evidence of his personal interest in the endeavors of those under him. The influence of interest upon successful achievement is so great as to require the studied attention of leaders.

(b) ***Self-respect* lies at the roots of all the higher instincts, and furnishes a foundation for the kind of inspiration a leader needs to give to those under him.** Without a man possess self-respect no appeal to him, [*sic*] except of the most sordid and selfish origin, will awaken any higher response. A military organization composed of such men would surely disintegrate, unless held together by the most iron discipline based on fear and spoils.

It is almost universal practice to stimulate the development of self-respect by requiring men to keep themselves and their surroundings clean and neat; to maintain a smart carriage and manner; and to comport themselves respectably. This has a sound basis in the peculiar psychological principle that what attributes men habitually pretend to have they will actually acquire. Progress is doubtless often slow and imperfect, but nevertheless is real; and when assisted by public opinion and stimulated by the force of example it is usually rapid. Herein we see the reason for the emphasis laid on these seemingly trivial, but really very important, matters in all highly efficient services. Through generations of experience they have learned this fundamental lesson.

All ranks and ratings would doubtless take kindly to the necessarily irksome and constant task of keeping up external appearances, if they appreciated better the genuine need for it. The profound influence of example, and of the opinion of others, in these matters imposes upon officers the important duty of themselves setting a good example of neatness, smartness and deportment; and of creating general opinion within the service in support of high standards in these respects.

A good leader will studiously avoid assailing the self-respect of his subordinates; by requiring lowering duties of them, by his manner towards them, or in other ways. He will on the contrary seek every means and occasion for developing their self-respect.

The pleasurable feeling of self-satisfaction and the human trait of pride furnish excellent self-respect builders. Praise and reward when merited, if utilized with judgment and moderation, are very useful to increase men's pride and satisfaction in their work and in themselves. It is good practice to be punctilious about giving due credit to men who have performed a special task well. Many other methods of fostering pride and self-respect will suggest themselves in the course of routine duty to officers who desire to make the most out of this method of giving needed inspiration to their men.

(c) **Esprit de corps** is based on collective self-respect; which furnishes a higher form of inspiration than does individual self-respect, because it is less selfish.

The relationship between *esprit* and loyalty is exceedingly close. One cannot exist without the other; they progress hand in hand. We cannot have adequate cohesion or coordination without loyalty and we cannot have effective loyalty without *esprit de corps*.

Good tradition is a great aid to *esprit* and is too much neglected in the navy; which should profit by the superior example of the marines in this respect. Men and officers should be made more familiar with the notable deeds of their predecessors in the navy, and in their own ships, or ships of the same name.

Competition offers one of the most useful means of stimulating pronounced pride and *esprit de corps*. Good leaders make it their habit to introduce the element of competition whenever practicable; between gun crews, boat crews, turret crews, divisions, watches, ships, or any other units which organization or circumstances shape into the semblance of a "team." Competition is all the more effective when successful efforts result; but even when a unit is frequently beaten its benefits will not be lost if officers take pains to point out evidences of improvement and to give encouragement for better efforts in the future.

When recruits are being handled, either in competitions or in ordinary work, the repeated suggestion that they are making constant progress has an excellent effect in creating *esprit* and in promoting the desired progress. Necessarily some criticism cannot be avoided with inefficient men, and it is a mistake to fail in frankness with them; but the practice of offering them nothing but criticism, more especially when couched in such tone or language as to offend their self-respect, individually or collectively, is ruinous to *esprit,* and is a certain indication that the officer so doing is not a leader. It is essential that a habit of pride and confidence be created; and this can be done only by repeated praise and encouragement.

An organization permeated with a firm belief in its own abilities is stimulated to undertake cheerfully much more difficult and daring tasks and to exert greater efforts to accomplish them, than if such confidence was lacking. Obviously, then, *esprit* is an element of great military value. It is important for leaders to understand that *esprit* is an abstract conviction of excellence, rather than the concrete excellence, and has a strong coloring of vanity in it. Men must be made to believe in their organizations' efficiency; probably to a greater degree, but certainly no less, than is justified by the facts.

Esprit can also serve many commonplace uses. It is said that at one period the higher command of the American Expeditionary Forces in France were greatly concerned over the serious congestion of the roads due to disregard of the traffic regulations. The ordinary road signs appeared to have no effect and the only solution seemed to be to increase greatly the traffic police force, at the expense of the trenches. A free use of the sign "Play the game!" posted near the traffic signs, proved an effective solution of the difficulty. The success of this simple appeal was due to the high *esprit* and loyalty of the American Expeditionary Forces.

Another example of utilizing *esprit*, while at the same time stimulating it, is given by the following quotation from a sign posted conspicuously near the gangway of a destroyer tender:

> Yes, you can have it
> If we haven't got it, we'll get it
> If we can't get it, we'll make it
> What is it?

To a marked degree *esprit de corps* is a measure of the spirit of the officers. None but they can create it; only they can easily destroy it. It is no unimportant part of the duty of officers to build up their organization spirit by studied suggestion at every opportunity, and by unremittingly scrupulous example.

The inspiration resulting from *esprit* has an important bearing on all forms of efficiency, and is cumulative in its effects. *Esprit* promotes special endeavor and therefore high efficiency. Successful achievement in its turn creates pride in, respect for and loyalty to one's organization, and hence still higher *esprit*.

(d) **Patriotism.**—Considering the oath taken by all officers on accepting their commissions, there can be no question but that officers who refrain from inculcating high patriotism in their subordinates commit a grave breach of faith and moral duty. This is obvious; but what is not so clear is that such neglect also denotes inefficient Leadership; in that the important source of inspiration to be found in loyalty to a high cause is not utilized.

Loyalty to a cause is the highest and most effective form of emotional inspiration. It will spur men on to undertake more difficult tasks, to exert greater efforts, to endure greater suffering, and to make greater sacrifices than any other incentive. The higher the cause, the more idealism it embodies, the greater will be the incitement. Excepting religion, there is contained in patriotism the highest and most idealistic cause that can animate man. Past history abounds in examples of the extraordinary inspiration due to patriotism. The future will offer an even greater impulse; since recent events have demonstrated that nationalism must survive if anarchy is to be avoided, and the greatest good to the greatest number is to be ensured. Such a cause is capable of inspiring the highest loyalty.

Even if neglectful of his moral duty actively to promote and foster patriotism among subordinates, an officer who is a good leader will not fail to utilize patriotism as an instrument of Leadership. An appeal to patriotism, where it can be used appropriately, will rarely fail to bring spontaneous response; once loyalty to the country, its institutions, and its ideals has been firmly established in men's hearts.

The American officer is prone to be diffident before his men about so sentimental a thing as patriotism, and to take it for granted that their patriotism is sufficient for the practical needs of the navy and Leadership. Considering the youth of our men, their heterogeneous racial character, and the great amount of Bolshevik and other pernicious propaganda that has been disseminated recently, it appears to be necessary for officers to undertake seriously the inculcation of patriotism.

Loyalty to any cause presupposes inner conviction of its justice and efficacy, and firm belief in the ideals for which it stands. Our men must be made to understand that the sane development of American institutions is the hope of humanity, and that such development is not possible unless stability and security are afforded the country by an efficient army and navy; which are under a solemn obligation, at all costs, to safeguard and further the country's interests at home and abroad whenever called upon to do so.

A valuable means of promoting patriotism is offered by inspiring tradition, in which American naval, military, and political history is rich. Few of our men are sufficiently familiar with this history to cause a pronounced feeling of patriotism towards the country. They should be thoroughly acquainted with the inspiring facts; and if the best results are to be obtained these should be brought to their attention repeatedly, because repetition is one of the strongest factors in creating a habit of thought.

Above all officers themselves must set an example of fine patriotism; scrupulously respecting the flag, and taking every occasion, by word and deed, to stand for America.

Patriotism, together with Interest, Self-respect and *Esprit de Corps*[,] are four principal agencies through which men receive the inspiration needed to meet adequately the unusual exigencies of military life. An equally important element of inspiration is the example of the leader, but since this factor is very potent in all other aspects of Leadership it assumes the importance of a cardinal principle.

Principle IV

THE LEADER'S EXAMPLE AND CHARACTER ARE THE MOST POTENT ELEMENTS IN LEADERSHIP

In exercising Control, in creating Psychological Harmony, and in inducing a needful measure of Emotional Inspiration, the value of the example of the leader can hardly be overestimated. This is largely due to the fact that his position renders him so conspicuous that every act constitutes a suggestion to others; and the influence of repeated suggestion upon crowds is very great.

The leader should personify the principles for which he stands; the captain or executive who lies abed until noon cannot expect the ship to be cleaned in the morning watch. If officers are slack their subordinates are sure to follow suit; if they practice what they preach, the struggle to make subordinates live up to the same principles is furthered tremendously.

In addition to the example of conduct, bearing and appearance which it is so necessary to set, one who aspires to be a leader must possess certain attributes of character; developed to a much higher degree than is required for proficiency in lower ratings. Before proceeding to a consideration of these character attributes, it is well to reflect that character development is a slow and tedious process requiring persistent effort. The earlier it is begun the greater will be the ultimate development.

The subject of military character is too broad and complex to be treated fully within the scope of this paper. All that can be attempted here is to furnish an outline upon which a reflective officer may formulate an adequate conception of the attributes most needful of development in his own particular case.

The essential qualities of character required by leaders segregate themselves naturally into three principal classes.

1. Basic attributes of individual efficiency.
2. Attributes pertaining to cooperation.
3. Combative qualities needed to cope with an enemy.

Let us consider these in sequence.

1. ***Basic Attributes of Individual Efficiency.***—If the respect and confidence of subordinates are to be commanded, a mind, which is to think for and direct them, should be an efficient mind; and this means developed mental capacity in many respects. The decision, which precedes every order, should be a sound decision; it should have a background of good knowledge and memory; and should be based on accurate observation and reasoning processes, both of which presuppose well-developed powers of application and concentration Very often decisions must be made quickly; hence a capacity for quick thinking is exceedingly useful to officers. Many circumstances require good imagination if due foresight and resourcefulness are to be exercised; imagination is the great creative agent and needs to be highly developed in officers. A correct decision will frequently need the quality of understanding, which has its origin in judgment and a sense

of proportion and reality. Finally the officer must possess a strong will, so that he will surely order done what his mind tells him is the correct decision, and will adhere to such decision in the face of subsequent obstacles.

The foregoing qualities of mental capacity should be combined with high ideals. "Honor, virtue, patriotism, and subordination" are prescribed by custom and regulations; to which should be added high ideals of loyalty, justice and duty. An intellectual rogue is as undesirable in a military organization as a stupid saint. An officer must embody the reverse combination if his individual efficiency is to meet the requirements of his position.

2. *Attributes Bearing on Cooperation.*—It is not enough that each officer or man shall possess only those attributes which render him individually proficient. In armies and navies one of the most prominent and governing conditions is that great numbers of men are thrown into close association, and that their efforts require to be harmonized, and coordinated, if success is to be attained. Minor friction between personalities may readily prevent due cooperation, and reduce the capacity for useful collective effort to a dangerous minimum.

First let us consider a group of cooperation qualities, which may be generally classified as *Social Attributes*. The fundamental basis of harmonious association with others is *Charity;* which is manifested by unselfishness, sympathy, consideration, and tolerance. Besides charity the quality of *Sociability* is of great use in promoting harmonious association. Sociability includes civility and a sense of obligation to the community; it is promoted further by amiability and volubility, and to a marked degree by sprightliness, cheerfulness, and humor. In addition to Charity and Sociability human experience demonstrates that a degree of *Polish* is essential to the permanence of harmonious association. One cannot be too unconventional without giving offence to some who may misunderstand his motives and intentions. Good manners are a much safer and more rational rule of intercourse, since they have a universally accepted meaning. Polish also presupposes sufficient *savoir faire* to give a degree of assurance and tact without which sociability is marred greatly. The foregoing *Social Attributes* embodied in Charity, Sociability and Polish are indispensable to harmonious intercourse and cooperation.

Another class of attributes bearing on cooperation may be grouped under the heading *Personality*. Foremost in this class is personal magnetism, which is probably less susceptible of cultivation than any other quality of military character. Yet its development is so important as to call for special efforts. Poise and prestige are also needed to round out a good military personality, and their acquisition will also further the development of personal charm and magnetism. Poise and prestige go a long way towards creating in the minds of subordinates a belief in the leader's fitness to command them.

The third group of qualities needful in cooperation may be called *Expressive Attributes*. Obviously a leader must express to his subordinates clearly and effectively his ideas and orders if his men are to interpret them accurately, intelligently, and coordinately. A leader should be at ease when talking to a crowd, and be able to express himself with facility, either orally or in writing. Otherwise it will be impossible to get into other heads what is inside his own head, and coordination necessarily will be hampered.

Coordination is one of the cardinal factors of efficiency in every field of naval and military activity. The three groups of character qualities considered above, Social Attributes, Personality, and the Expressive Attributes, all have a vital influence upon a leader's ability to get cooperation among his subordinates. It is necessary to consider, finally, the:

3. ***Combative Qualities Needed to Cope with an Enemy.***— Hostile operations require first of all that leaders be pugnacious.

Pugnacity implies a degree of arrogance towards an enemy. It includes courage; which normally is not so much a question of character as it is a product of conditions—feelings of confidence in strength and efficiency, high morale, etc. Pugnacity presupposes great determination; together with self-reliance and decision. It includes abundant activity, as well as boldness, dash and ardor.

The great balance wheel to pugnacity is *Steadiness*. Coolness and clear-mindedness under tension are especially desirable in one who must make the responsible decisions. To carry plans through in the face of inevitable discouragements there are required hopeful buoyancy and much patience; besides highly developed endurance—both physical vigor and mental persistence. All these give steadiness.

Pugnacity with steadiness combine the principal combative characteristics, essential to cope with an enemy.

This completes the necessarily brief outline of the qualities most desirable in the military character.

Let us sum up the elements of Leadership. The basic principle is:

I. A leader must exercise control over his subordinates.

Control requires first of all, *discipline* [for example], instinctive obedience—and second, mechanical *drill.*

These agencies facilitate control not only in ordinary circumstances but also under the adverse influences presented by emergencies; and are established primarily through the medium of habit. A third factor in control is the proficiency of the leader in utilizing practically the power of *Suggestion.*

It is necessary that a leader shall establish supremacy over his subordinates through the above means; yet equally necessary that their inner hostility be not incurred. A paradox is avoided through the second principle, namely,

II. Psychological harmony within an organization is indispensable to its general efficiency.

Such harmony is obtained primarily through (a) a general belief in the prevalence of justice; (b) understanding on the part of subordinates of the need for the troublesome requirements of naval life and current work; (c) a spirit of comradeship, avoiding undue familiarity, between all ranks, and (d) adequate provision for interesting recreation.

The principle of psychological harmony is allied closely to that of control. They afford each other mutual support, and together furnish a good foundation for Leadership. Yet a third element is necessary, to avoid apathy and to supply an impulse for special effort.

III. Some degree of emotional inspiration is essential to the highest efficiency.

The most valuable agencies at the disposal of leaders, to give needful inspiration, are (a) interest, which may furnish a strong incentive under all circumstances; (b) self-respect, which is at the root of all the higher feelings; (c) *esprit de corps* (collective self-respect), which supplies constant inspiration for special effort and achievement by an organization; and (d) patriotism, a cause to which all can give the highest loyalty.

A capable leader will develop and make use of all these inspiring aids to the highest efficiency of his subordinates, and will utilize also to the same end the influence of example. The importance of the latter is so great in its bearing upon all three of the preceding principles as to constitute a fourth cardinal principle of Leadership.

IV. The leader's example and character are the most potent elements in Leadership.

The force of the leader's example results from his being so conspicuous that his bearing and actions become constant suggestions for imitation by those under him. The example set necessarily depends to a great degree upon the leader's character. Military Character has three primary subdivisions: (1) Attributes of *individual efficiency,* whose principal components are ideals and mental capacity; (2) qualities bearing on *cooperation,* which comprise social attributes, personality, and expressive ability; and (3) the *combative* attributes, which are a compound mainly of pugnacity and steadiness.

A thorough understanding of the foregoing principles, together with facility in their practical application, is required of any officer before he can fulfill his primary role of a leader.

FOUR

Forgetting the Lessons of History

Knox recognized that unlike the land or air forces of the U.S. Army, the U.S. Navy had the distinctive capacity to perform a unique peacetime mission in global affairs. Army and air forces required land bases from which to operate, whereas navies operated in the global commons whether in peace or war. For this reason, discussions centering primarily on technical dimensions or the practical application of military tactics failed to measure against the strategic perspectives articulated by American naval professionals like Dudley W. Knox, Ernest J. King, and William S. Pye. In their collective assessment, the "naval profession is the most varied in the world. . . . The naval officer requires a working knowledge of many branches of human endeavor."[1] Drawing on lessons from the First World War, Knox recognized that the Navy had ventured into previously uncharted waters, which would require larger-scale strategic thinking. The competition for global resources required a fresh discussion among the maritime powers. In particular, the Royal Navy and Imperial Japanese Navy appeared as potential allies—or perhaps as fundamental enemies. Following the Washington Naval Conference of 1922–23, British and Japanese forces provided means to measure future concepts of American naval policy.

In general the U.S. Navy frowned upon officers who broke the cloistered ranks of the service to engage the public on questions of American policy or maritime strategy. Knox largely followed protocol by restricting his arguments to the U.S. Naval Institute *Proceedings*. However, he also hoped to engage a wider audience. The

U.S. Navy had initially provided Knox with inspiration, but the constraints of the service began to wear on him after the First World War. Like other Naval Academy graduates, Knox considered his Navy commission a lifetime commitment. He earned an accelerated wartime promotion to the rank of captain, which congressional legislation made permanent in 1919. In this rank, Knox prepared for a sleepy career, with the clear understanding of limited prospects for promotion in the overfilled ranks of the postwar Navy. He assumed command of the flagship of the Pacific Fleet in 1920, only to receive orders in 1921 to decommission the aging USS *Brooklyn*. Knox then assumed command of another antique, the *Charleston*, which was also decommissioned shortly thereafter.

Knox accepted the likelihood of retiring at the rank of captain with few prospects for a seagoing command leading to admiralty. Unlike King, who abandoned the battleship ranks for a career in submarines, Knox decided to pursue broader horizons. With more than twenty-three years before the mast, Knox requested transfer to the U.S. Navy Retired List. At that time, the list provided opportunities for Navy personnel to pursue professional aspirations outside the service. Officers maintained permanent commissioned status in the rolls of the Navy, which provided inroads to continue service in a retired status. Upon transfer to the Retired List in November 1921, Knox accepted a civil service appointment as the director of the Office of Naval Records. He also maintained his retired rank as a captain. After retirement, he frequently traveled between the Navy Department in Washington and the Naval War College in Newport.

Out of uniform, Knox continued to serve the interests of the service by focusing on improving the educational foundations of the Navy. The Naval War College president, Sims, invited Knox to deliver lectures on strategy and the role of doctrine in naval operations for students at the college. Knox retained a stiff military posture in the classroom, periodically peering over the bridge of his wire spectacles to the listening students. Knox guided the students through discussions of past wars, analyzing the factors that influenced decisions of pivotal battles, yet he avoided the empirical approach and rarely offered students a clear "staff school" solution. Among the more skeptical listeners in the classroom was Capt. Thomas C. Hart, who wondered whether studies of past

wars continued to hold contemporary relevance within the technical context of aviation and submarines. "Listened to quite a medi-
ocre lecture from 'Baldy' Knox this afternoon," Hart noted in his
diary in January 1923.[2]

Knox encouraged students to examine the circumstances and
the intangible factors of personality to gain an informed approach
to contemporary challenges. He viewed historical scholarship as a
weapon in the Navy's arsenal that strategists frequently failed to
consider. He challenged Navy professionals to embrace their
responsibility as the caretakers of the service, as the heirs to a
heroic maritime tradition, and as defenders of the United States in
both peace and war. Knox further noted the unfinished Navy
Department project to collect and transcribe the original records
of the Union and Confederate navies, which had stalled during
the First World War. He volunteered to restart the effort, which the
Navy Department eventually published as *Official Records of the
Union and Confederate Navies in the War of the Rebellion* in 1926. That
same year, Knox helped organize the Naval Historical Foundation.

The Naval Historical Foundation provided a platform for the
Navy to rally the American public. In advancing a firmly global
vision of American sea power, Knox drew assistance from a fellow
Naval War College graduate from the class of 1913, retired U.S.
Marine colonel Frederick H. Delano, whose father, Rear Adm.
Francis H. Delano, also had close family associations with Franklin
Delano Roosevelt. With direct assistance from the Delano and the
Roosevelt families, Knox helped expand the role of the Naval Historical Foundation. Through organizations like the Naval Historical Foundation, Navy League, and Naval Order of the United
States, Knox and Roosevelt worked behind the scenes to fuse their
interests in maritime history with more practical efforts to frame a
strategy designed to maintain the Navy during a period of limited
budgets, partisan infighting within Congress, and foreign conflict
in the 1930s.

OUR VANISHING HISTORY AND TRADITIONS

1926

The early history of any great nation is not only of especial interest to succeeding generations, but also of vital constructive value to the progress of the world, because the youthful virile stage of development most clearly marks the fundamental forces which have been at work. When we look forward several hundred years and vision the maturity of the United States—her magnitude in all things material and her leadership in all things cultural and spiritual—we begin to realize how important it is to the advancement of civilization that the record of the origins and early development of this potential giant of a country should be carefully preserved.

A great deal is now being done to this end in many fields of American history, but, unfortunately, much less in the naval field than in any other one of importance. The influence of naval and maritime affairs upon the course of the nation's history has been very much greater than can possibly be recognized by the average person. This is, undoubtedly, largely due to glaring deficiencies in our written naval history, which in their turn arise from the extraordinary inaccessibility of authentic sources.

The general condition is best illustrated by reference to the Revolutionary War, in which it has been claimed that we had more sailors engaged than soldiers. At all events the spontaneous uprising on the sea was on a scale quite comparable to that ashore. Its general character has been described by [U.S. Navy Reserve captain Thomas G. Frothingham], Secretary of the Massachusetts Military Historical Society in the following words:

> The dogged resistance of the Americans was maintaining this successful defense at home in the face of military defeats in set battles, and, in addition, it must be kept in mind that, with the British thus brought to an *impasse* in the American colonies, the Americans themselves were able to carry on an offensive, which was doing decisive harm to Great Britain. It is a fact that the real offensive of the American colonies was on the sea, where the American privateers were taking such an unprecedented toll of British commerce that these heavy losses to the British merchants were bringing about the demands in Parliament to let the Americans go. It is not generally understood, but our whole offensive strength, in the true military sense of doing damage to the enemy, was thus upon the sea, and the

widespread losses inflicted upon British commerce provided the argument for setting free an obstinate people, who not only had shown that they refused to submit on the land, but also continued to destroy shipping in increasing totals on the sea. In a military sense, this meant that the Americans were inflicting heavy damage upon the British, while the British were finding themselves unable to do damage to the Americans.

We are compelled to the conclusion that a military situation like this could not exist through all the years of trial, unless there was a strong surge underneath. Such a determined resistance of a people must mean a mighty impelling force. We must recognize this military test as proving that the rising of our ancestors was one of the instinctive primitive movements of a people which can be brought about only where long continued causes have produced the inevitable effect of creating an irresistible force. This force was the spirit of our ancestors, created by their inborn instinct for self-government, and this should be emphasized at our coming anniversary observances.

The importance of the naval side (including irregular forces) of the Revolution is manifest. Why has no comprehensive history of all this naval activity ever been written? The explanation is very simple. Many of the records, of course, have been lost, but hundreds of thousands of others still in existence are so badly scattered as to make it almost impossible to find and collate the information which they contain and to piece together anything approaching a complete history of what occurred. Fortunately there are a number of large collections of Revolutionary documents in state archives and in the files of historical societies and libraries. But probably the greater number are distributed in small groups among thousands of small libraries, county courthouses, small historical societies, and private collectors.

Recognizing this unsatisfactory situation, Congress appropriated $30,000 in 1913 for the purpose of photographing the scattered Revolutionary military and naval documents and making a federal collection of copies, which would be sufficiently complete to serve historical needs. The commission, which started this work, very soon decided that their funds would limit efforts to a few states, and decided to concentrate upon Massachusetts, Virginia, and North Carolina. Even in this restricted field it was found impossible to be thorough. For example, all that could be done in Massachusetts was to photostat from the state archives the Massachusetts Board of War minutes, orders, and letters (2,914 documents) and from the Harvard University Library, [Henry] Hamilton's Journal of the Vincennes Expedition (77 documents). In the Harvard Library alone, to say nothing of hundreds of other sources of Revolutionary material within the state of Massachusetts, there must remain thousands of documents which could not be copied. The commission ceased its work in 1914 on account of exhaustion of funds.

Whether Congress will ever renew appropriations for the completion of the task of collecting originals or copies of Revolutionary historical documents is doubtful. The necessity of doing so much photostating makes the work expensive, which difficulty might be largely overcome by the use of some such device as the recent invention of Admiral [Bradley] Fiske permitting the ready reading of extremely small type, and therefore a great reduction in the size of the photostat copy. Meantime efforts are being made to include private collectors to donate originals or copies of Revolutionary manuscript and pictures, and in this way, considerable progress recently has been made in building up the naval archives. New material is constantly coming to light. Only within the last few days the writer learned of three groups of very early manuscript, one of them containing about 1,000 documents, which have been in a garret or otherwise inaccessible for more than a hundred years. Every effort is being made to obtain at least copies of these before they are accidentally burned or sold and scattered to the four winds.

One might imagine that after the adoption of the Constitution and the formation of the existing federal government, pains were taken to keep reasonably complete official naval files. But such is unfortunately not true. The case is illustrated by the recent discovery of an official report made in 1815 by the Board of Navy Commissioners to the Secretary of the Navy, by special request of the latter. This important document making a general survey and broad recommendations respecting the whole naval establishment—navy yards, ships, personnel, laws, and so forth—remained in the possession of descendants of one of the Board of Navy Commissioners until very recently when it was donated to the public archives. This is merely one of a great number of similar cases, which could be cited to demonstrate the wide dispersion and deplorable inaccessibility of the official sources of naval history and tradition; a condition resulting from old customs rather than any culpability on the part of individuals.

In the old days there was nothing approaching modern filing systems or regulations regarding official correspondence and records. Personal idiosyncrasy more than any other factor governed both the method of filing and the final disposition of papers, and it has been said that there were few qualities which the "old-timers" were more famous for than a degree of eccentricity. The fact that commanding officers often had financial responsibilities in connection with their duties was doubtless a large influence in the custom of considering what we now regard as official files as belonging to the officer himself. Upon the detachment of an officer of rank, he seems to have taken the files of his office with him, as a matter of course. This practice continued even after the Civil War. The thirty volume printed *Official Records of the Union and Confederate Navies* could not have been made even approximately complete without reference to the thousands of originally official documents in the personal possession of nearly every officer, who had served in command rank during the Civil War.

Many large collections of this kind were temporarily loaned to the Navy Department for the purpose of being copied, preliminary to printing, and then returned to the owner. All papers could not be printed. Fortunately some of the most important large collections, such as the [David G.] Farragut, [David D.] Porter, [John] Dalghren, [Louis M.] Goldsborough, [Charles H.] Davis, [Josiah] McKean, [William] Mervine, [William F.] Wise, and [David] Macomb papers were donated and are now carefully preserved in the official archives. Others were placed on indefinite loan and in that status have been at least available for reference for a number of years, though when the owners or their heirs wish them back, the Government will be in the anomalous position of having to give up to private individuals what are in fact the originals of official historical records. In the course of a few generations most of such papers in private hands are inevitably burned, rat-eaten, lost, rotted, scattered, or sold to persons whose addresses are difficult to determine. Naval history and tradition vanish with them.

But history and tradition are by no means limited to what may be contained in official correspondence. Personal letters very often give more interesting sidelights and greater detail to important affairs. As a reflection of the morale, discipline, manner of living, and customs, they are incomparable. They are the best source of establishing the vital element of the "state of mind" of naval personnel during war and peace. From a large number of personal letters from "Lion-hearted" [Charles W.] Flusser to his mother and sister, who very kindly donated them to the official archives, the following matter is selected as illustrating these points.

> . . . I have tried to do everything for the cause here, but obstinacy, prejudice, and laziness, on our side have defeated nearly all. I feel confident that I could have this state in the Union at this time had I had the distribution and control of the Army and Naval Forces down here. I have written and recommended till I am tired and disgusted, and only wish my letters were

public instead of unofficial. If my advice had been acted on we might now have several loyal regiments of North Carolinians in the field. . . .

. . . Remember, Mama, all this is entre nous, sub rosa, etc., etc. The above is terribly egotistical, but I am pleased with my egotism when writing to you—for to you I like to write my thoughts as they are, and not as other men hear them expressed.

. . . I was interrupted by the music of the band of the 46th Massachusetts Regiment which came off to serenade me. I had to invite them on board. They gave us some music to which the men danced and sang songs which they enjoyed hugely.

. . . Do not believe any stories you hear of my exposing myself. I shall try to keep my life for you. I hope 1 shall never be afraid to go where duty calls, and I pray God to give me courage before going into battle, (without this I think I should be a coward) but I do not think I have ever exposed my life recklessly. A man can have little to live for, must be very miserable, who commits suicide in that way. My men are not cowards—they need no rash example to make them fight. They combat for a good cause, and for the reputation the boat has already attained. They are proud of her and I of them. They are sad scamps, but they will fight.

. . . I went out the other day with a flag of truce and had a pleasant interview with a Lieutenant Colonel [Randolph] Townes of the 62nd Georgia. . . . I bantered him pleasantly and he me. I carried out to him some good whisky, and tolerable cigars. I told him I knew he had had nothing of the sort for a long time. From the way he "took to" them I think my surmise was correct. He laughed at the idea of our starving the Rebs into submission. There will certainly be a famine in this state—no one left here to cultivate the crops. Provisions are scarce and very dear. Alas for the poor!

We met the enemy on the tenth instant, a short distance below the Elizabeth [River], and protected by a four-gun battery. They had five steamers; we had nine, but only two or three of ours got up in time to fight the rebel steamers.

I was given the lead. I singled out the largest vessel, Commodore [William F.] Lynch's flagship, the steamer *Sea Bird*, and ordered my pilot to run her down.

When about two hundred yards from her, and after passing through the fire of the battery and giving them some good shots in return, I fired a nine-inch shell at her, which struck her just amidships, at the water line, passing through her as if she was so much paper, and exploded a great distance beyond. I then called away boarders and ran for her, my men picking up their muskets, pistols and cutlasses for a hand-to-hand fight. When fifty yards or more from her she hauled down her flag and her commander appeared on the upper deck holding open his coat to signify that he had surrendered. I immediately ordered the helm put a-port and the steamer stopped to avoid striking him, but my men were so crazy with excitement and made so much noise that the helmsman could not hear, and so plump into her we went, smashing in her whole port bow. My men immediately jumped on board and I had to follow to restrain them from injuring the prisoners. The captain surrendered to my vessel, stated that he was in a sinking condition, and asked me to rescue his officers and men. I was anxious to secure another steamer and gave the order to back out and pursue when, to my inexpressible annoyance, I found that as we struck the *Sea Bird* the fastenings of our anchor went and the anchor had gone to the bottom, so we were anchored and I could not move. The men were frantic with excitement, and for ten minutes I could not get anyone to slip the chain, then one of the engineers unshackled it. I cut the line which fastened us to our prize with my sword, and was just leaving when her captain came to me for the second or third time and begged me, for God's sake, not to leave his men to drown; so to save them I reluctantly gave up the pursuit. While I was at anchor engaged taking the prisoners from the sinking vessel two small rebel steamers ran around me, firing with musketry at my men. I could have sunk them both with one gun each, but my men were so wild that I could not get them to their quarters at the great guns. One of these steamers came up on my starboard quarter, only ten or fifteen yards off, where there was not a man but myself, and tried to train a great gun on us. I repeatedly called the men to their guns, but they would not come, so as a last chance, for I felt that if the gun was fired I was destroyed, I drew my revolver, a small-sized Colt's, and fired at the captain of the enemy's gun. I fired three or four shots with deliberate aim and saw the captain of the gun and the man on his left fall; whether I hit them or not I do not know, I only know that the gun was not fired.

Personal letters which deal with naval life and naval affairs are undoubtedly a very valuable source of naval history and tradition and have an important place in official archives, since they shed much light upon official reports of every nature. In the past there has been less attention to this class of documents than their real value warrants, and the number available for examination is correspondingly small. The reluctance which many persons feel to violating the privacy of personal letters by placing them in public archives can always be obviated by special arrangements for safeguarding their confidential nature until after the passage of several generations, or other specified time.

The foregoing is intended mainly to indicate the existing danger of losing permanently some of our most valuable naval history and tradition because of the very wide dispersion of manuscript sources. This condition renders it practically impossible to collate the needful information for any comprehensive works on naval history which will do justice to the Navy and the nation, and, moreover, greatly adds to the probability of destruction of the documents. It is manifestly desirable that such valuable records should be accumulated into a few large collections, systematically archived, and properly secured against fire and other risks.

Perhaps the greatest forward step which could now be taken to this end is the erection of the government archive building in Washington, which already has been authorized by Congress, but for which construction funds still remain to be appropriated. The completion of such a building would seem certain to stimulate public interest in the general question of the preservation of historical records and to persuade many private collectors to deposit historical manuscript in the great central archives. A further advantage will be provision for adequate space in which to make accessible in a systematic way huge quantities of old manuscript now boxed up and stored by the several government departments in basements and numerous other odd places. For example, large numbers of documents pertaining to naval history are now contained in the store rooms of the State, War, Treasury, and other departments. Similarly each of the various bureaus and offices of the Navy Department, many of the branch offices and naval stations outside of Washington, and many of the American Consulates abroad, have quantities of "dead" and forgotten files of no administrative value which properly belong in the central archives. The writer has been told of a recent "find" of naval manuscript pertaining to the Barbary War in the files of the Consulate of Algiers.

But the completion of a national archive building does not seem probable for a number of years. Meantime the Navy Department is making efforts toward getting its own historical documents in some kind of order. About thirty-five years ago the "dead" files of the Secretary of the Navy up to 1885 were transferred to the Office of Naval Records and now form the nucleus of the Navy's historical archives. After this first step little was done in the way of archiving (many papers being received but merely stored) until after the World

War when Congress appropriated money for collecting, filing, and indexing naval documents pertaining to that war. While the World War papers are being thus archived a simultaneous effort is also being made to fill in the gap between 1885 and 1917, and further to add to the archives of older date, many papers previously overlooked or subsequently accumulated. It is estimated that that the Office of Naval Records now contains about one million documents of dates previous to 1885, and is thus much the largest single depository for old naval manuscript in the country.

However diligent the Navy Department may be in bringing together and archiving such records as are now in the custody of branches of the naval establishment and of other government departments, it can never adequately safeguard our early history and tradition without the interest and aid of officers and the relatives of former officers. Old documents are too widely scattered and their location too little known to permit the discovery of any great number of them without the constant watchfulness of a large number of persons. Only a few weeks ago, while motoring near Narragansett Pier, the writer accidentally stopped at an old farmhouse and quite unexpectedly found in the front parlor the naval historical document of the War of 1813 reproduced on another page herein. When the owner's attention was called to its historical value he was kind enough to have it photo-stated at his own expense and the copy forwarded to the Navy Department. It is in such ways that the service could be helpful in building up the central source of our history.

There also are other ways. In almost every naval family of maturity there are to be found papers which would be of much value to the official archives. The importance of personal letters containing references to naval life and incidents has been pointed out above. In addition the private files often include diaries and copies of important official reports, the originals of which may have been lost. For example, two years ago an inquiry from a participant in the first Boxer Relief Expedition of 1900 led to a search being made for the official report of the commander of the American contingent. Documents of so late a date not having yet been turned over to the Office of Records, reference was made to the original bureau files, but the report could not be found. There was evidence of the original report having been received and lost and the commandant at Cavite having been asked to forward a duplicate. If he did so, the duplicate also was lost. Inquiry was then made of other participants for data, and Captain Courtney very kindly donated his private diary, which as subsequent events proved contained photographs and many details not included in the official report. After a two-year search a copy of the latter was finally discovered among the private papers of one of the heirs of its author.

A similar case is that of the naval operations at Vera Cruz in April and May of 1914. Very recent careful search of Navy and State Department files failed to disclose a single document pertaining to the naval landing and occupation of that city. The unfortunate custom, which has lately prevailed of burning ships' files of supposedly no historical value, probably means that there are no records of the important Vera Cruz operations except such as may remain among the personal papers of officers. In the Department's historical archives (not administrative files) they would be secure against loss.

It is easy to understand the reluctance which most persons feel over parting with family papers. But the sentimental aspects of this question appear to be outweighed by practical advantages to the owners themselves. The security of the precious documents is far greater when placed in public archives, where they are usually also more accessible for reference by members of the family. But perhaps the greatest advantage of all is that they are brought into close relation with a large number of other papers upon the same subjects, thus making possible a proper understanding of the comparatively few documents otherwise held out of the main collection. Among family papers there are often a few of outstanding personal interest, such as letters of commendation. In such cases a photostat copy is almost as satisfactory for the public archives as the original document. In all cases a photostat reproduction is much better than no copy at all for the Department's historical archives.

One of the greatest enemies of naval history is the private collector of manuscript and old pictures. Due to these faddists probably more historical records are now being dispersed beyond the reach of the research worker than are finding their way into large public collections. Almost every second-hand bookseller carries a stock of manuscript, and there are frequent sales at auction of much historically valuable material that was originally the equivalent of what we now consider as official files. Among papers recently seen in the stock of a second-hand dealer were some twenty official letter-books of the commander of a blockade squadron during the Civil War. Another dealer has for sale the official notification from the Secretary of the Navy to the commander-in-chief on the coast of California that the War with Mexico had terminated.

The old official documents are, of course, more badly needed to complete the official sources of history and tradition than any other kind of material. The older the documents, the greater will be their accession value since it is in our earlier history that the greatest gaps exist. From the beginning of the Revolution to the year 1798 is the most important period of all, not only because of its antiquity but also on account of a fire in 1800 which destroyed most of the files of the War Department, which had administered the Navy under the Constitution until 1798. Most naval officers are poorer even than the Office of Naval Records (which has no funds for the purchase of manuscript) and therefore can hardly be expected to aid the latter by buying in old naval manuscript. But they may have opportunities of discouraging the sale of old collections, or of having them photo-stated before being sold, or of encouraging some large library or historical society to buy them. A service will be done the Office of Naval Records by notifying it of the discovery of old historical material, so that at least a record of its existence and location may be kept.

Viewing the whole question broadly the rescue from loss and the subsequent preservation of our Navy's history and traditions depends primarily upon the degree of interest felt by naval officers and the relatives of former officers. If keen interest in the matter exists, official and unofficial ways and means will be exerted toward filling the great gaps in manuscript sources. Undoubtedly, the present lack of general interest is due to a misconception of the condition of the naval archives, which it is the principal purpose of this paper to correct.

The author of a recent book on old merchant marine affairs of this continent says: "I have been collecting information on the subject for many years. But owing to the fact that first-hand sources of information were rapidly vanishing, I have hastened the task of compilation in the hope that the publication of this record might result in an effort being made by public bodies to preserve whatever remains of interest and value in connection with the old-time shipping." His plea can be applied with equal justice to the case of our vanishing sources of naval history and traditions.

FIVE

The Navy as Peacemaker

From within the Navy Department, Knox orchestrated a campaign to educate fellow Navy officers about the influence of sea power on the history of the United States, and by the 1920s Franklin D. Roosevelt had taken a keen interest in Knox and his work. American maritime history provided a platform for Roosevelt to engage labor unions and industrialists, whose shipyards and railroads connected to industrial centers inland, providing the means to create new jobs in the effort to refit the Navy as a global force. Having secured the Democratic Party nomination to defeat Republican Herbert Hoover during the presidential election of 1933, Roosevelt pursued a novel maritime strategy of withdrawing American forces from the Philippines, expanding the peacetime deterrence function of the Navy, establishing the U.S. Marine Corps as an elite expeditionary force, and developing new warship classes—such as aircraft carriers and long-range submarines.

Together Roosevelt and Knox fused American domestic economic policy with the vision of a global peacetime mission for the Navy. In 1934 Roosevelt secured appropriations for the Navy under the Vinson-Trammell Act, which provided for warship construction and other improvements to Navy facilities. Roosevelt diverted funds appropriated under the act for Knox's efforts to compile histories of the Navy. Yet funding histories of the U.S. Navy seemed to violate the provisions of the act set by Congress, and the costs involved seemed exorbitant in comparison with the more immediate problems of the economic depression. The acting director of the Bureau of Budget, Daniel W. Bell, estimated that the Knox history project would require an estimated 114 volumes and a research budget in excess of $1 million—at that time a considerable sum.

But Roosevelt was insistent on the project's importance. "This is my pet child," he admitted to Bell. "Push the appropriation and try to make it a revolving fund."[1] Roosevelt also directed the first installment of money to be dedicated to assembling records associated with the "Quasi-War with France." In turn Bell questioned the basic focus of the project by reasoning that this "may be justified by reasons not known to me, but to a layman it would seem that the records of the World War or the Spanish-American War would be of greater interest and importance to the public and the Government than the records of wars that have almost been forgotten by most people."[2] It was clear that Roosevelt, in supporting an apparently esoteric research project about a widely forgotten war, recognized the strategic influence of history on the American public. His insistence that Knox refer to "quasi" wars of the past also provided an elegant point of reference in the future employment of Navy forces within the constraints of the neutrality acts of the 1930s.

Roosevelt and Knox collaborated to weave an argument for employing the Navy as a peacekeeping force, which focused upon safeguarding global economic interests and served as the first line in the maritime defense of the United States. This visionary interpretation of American sea power soothed critiques from pacifist organizations and, coincidentally, helped amplify the domestic policies of the Roosevelt administration. In correspondence forwarded to Roosevelt by Secretary of the Navy Claude Swanson, then director for the Endowment for International Peace, James Brown Scott wrote in January 1937 that the histories compiled by Knox "employed the happy phrase, 'quasi-war with France' and I imagine that the term which you have used will be adopted and remain." Scott continued: "The United States thus demonstrated determination to preserve their independence not merely at home but also on the high seas, in any and every part of the world."[3] As global tensions heightened into the 1930s with the emergence of Imperial Japanese expansion in China and Manchuria as well as Nazi and Fascist expansion in the Mediterranean and Europe, Roosevelt drew from the historical precedence of these quasi-war studies to explain his strategy to defend global American interests.

This strategy included deployment of U.S. Navy warships to foreign waters in peacetime. To communicate this idea, Roosevelt directed Knox to examine the early history of the U.S. Navy. Undeclared wars against the Barbary pirates and the French had provided the impetus within Congress to establish the U.S. Navy in 1794. By extension, the quasi-wars of the past provided a useful point of historical reference in explaining Roosevelt's maritime strategy for conducting quasi-wars of the future—using Navy warships to defend the global strategic interests of the United States while they also served as the first line of American defense on the high seas.

Sailing in the first six frigates of the newly created U.S. Navy, American bluejackets engaged in naval quasi-wars against the Barbary pirates and the postrevolutionary French navy to defend the maritime interests of the United States in distant European waters. To retell the heroic history of the Navy, Knox initiated an international campaign to compile, transcribe, and publish original records. In 1936 government funding provided the means to produce the final volume of *Naval Documents Related to the Quasi-War between the United States and France.* This collection appeared in libraries and bookshops at roughly the same time as a commercially published book by Knox, *A History of the United States Navy.* Roosevelt congratulated Knox on the latter work, which was widely described in literary reviews of the period as the "best one-volume history of the United States Navy in existence."[4]

Maritime history enabled Knox to explain his naval strategy to the American public. Embracing the neutrality acts of the 1930s, he invoked maritime precedence to employ the Navy, merchant marine, and the neutral flag of the United States. Within this context, Knox drafted the following essay, "Naval Power as a Preserver of Neutrality and Peace," in 1937. It revisited the basic thesis found in a 1914 essay by President Theodore Roosevelt, "The Navy as Peacekeeper."[5] By implication, Knox also connected the maritime strategies of both Teddy and Franklin Roosevelt for American readers. Published shortly before the Japanese sank the USS *Panay* (PR 5) in China, this 1937 essay by Knox rationalized the American strategy for employing the Navy in operations designed to engage foreign rivals, pursue partnerships, and safeguard peacetime global economic stability through the common entrepreneurial influence of sea power.

NAVAL POWER AS A PRESERVER OF
NEUTRALITY AND PEACE

1937

*To secure respect to a neutral flag requires a naval force, organized and ready to vindicate it
from insult or aggression. This may even prevent the necessity of going to war.*
Franklin Delano Roosevelt

How to preserve our neutrality peacefully during the next great war abroad,
without submitting to serious economic or political injury, is among the greater
questions which now concern earnest Americans. We are greatly perturbed by
the growing evidence of coming conflict on a vast scale in both Asia and
Europe. We fear the traditional menace of being drawn into a quarrel between
foreign belligerents because of grave damage to our just rights and general
interests, arising incidentally from their methods of warfare against each
other.

As of old, a large and influential group of citizens now hopes to solve this
dilemma by curtailing American potential fighting power. It would reduce our
military and naval forces, tether the munition makers, shipbuilders, bankers,
and others who might enjoy profits from our participation in war, and so alter
neutrality rules as to remove the stigma of illegality from a variety of belligerent actions under which America at peace would nevertheless suffer griev-
ously. The futility of weakness in preserving neutrality, or avoiding war on
account of breaches of neutrality, has been thoroughly demonstrated by our
history, not to mention the common experience of other nations. So true is
this, so palpably true, that a mere examination of the facts should be sufficient
to convince anyone whose judgment has its basis in reality and reason. If there
is any solution of the problem set forth it cannot lie in feebleness, but in the
opposite direction—in the realm of strong preparedness together with the
pacific persuasions of ready force.

Such a conclusion is also well fortified by the abundant examples offered
by history of the peaceful preservation of neutral rights and general interests
through the influence of military-naval power. In this respect a predominant
British Navy in the century preceding the World War afforded striking illustration, while our own Navy played a similar part on a smaller scale. The present
situation of seemingly impending war abroad therefore undoubtedly calls for
the strengthening of America's combat power, rather than its curtailment, if

we hope to avoid being embroiled and if we desire to safeguard our essential interests. For us this is an untried method of accomplishing such objects under the critically difficult circumstances of a general war in Europe, which many persons now regard as probable within a few years. Where weakness has repeatedly failed us, strength should be doubly worthy of trial.

No better proof can be found of the restraining influence of obviously effective neutral power than that given by the vacillations of Germany with respect to ruthless submarining during the World War. Before the final and fateful U-boat campaign that brought forth American belligerency there were several false starts during a period of two years. This long prelude was characterized throughout by the German High Command's fear of neutral might. Their chief concern in debating submarine war on shipping was over which neutrals might thereby be drawn into the war, and especially what force such neutrals might bring to bear as future opponents.

Not until January of 1917 did the German command feel strong enough to win out despite the added weight of probable new enemies. It was then positively estimated that the Kaiser's armies could hold fast on the Continent while the U-boats brought England to her knees, before effective American military-naval aid could appear in Europe. The grave injury to neutral rights and interests that followed was clearly and largely a consequence of supposed neutral weakness, relatively speaking. With greater strength the neutrals could certainly have maintained their own peace without enduring substantial harm.

As early as November of 1914, the German Navy had gained sufficient experience in submarine warfare to convince its leaders of the then surprisingly high potential value of this method of attack on shipping. Accordingly a definite proposal for such a campaign was made to the Chancellor. The disapproval of the latter was based purely on military and political expediency. According to Admiral [Rinehard] Scheer (in his *Germany's High Sea Fleet in the World War*):

> the question was not whether it should be done, but when it could be done without ruining our position. Such a measure as the U-boat blockade would react detrimentally upon the attitude of neutrals and our imports; it could only be employed without dangerous consequences when our military position on the Continent was so secure that there could be no doubt as to the ultimate outcome there, and the danger that the neutrals would join our opponents might be regarded as out of the question. At the moment these conditions did not exist.

Evidently at this time it was respect for neutral strength which alone assured neutrals of peace and justice. By February, 1915, Germany felt sufficiently strong to begin ruthless submarining against enemy shipping, with a warning that neutral vessels should keep clear of the declared war zone. Orders were issued against torpedoing neutral ships but there was too much difficulty in distinguishing them and many were torpedoed.

Their safety really depended upon their keeping out of the zone, which the Germans vainly hoped they would do. Among neutrals the United States made the most vigorous protests, based largely on humanitarian grounds but accompanied by threats of declaring war. After the RMS *Lusitania* was sunk in May the German government was persuaded to forbid the torpedoing of all big passenger steamers, but the submarining of the SS *Arabic* in August, when the *U-24* felt she was acting in self-defense, further emphasized the difficulties of continuing the campaign under the restrictions against attacks on neutral shipping and passenger steamers.

This incident led to cessation of the war on shipping, except in the Mediterranean where Italy had come into the war and the danger from neutral susceptibilities was much less. It should be remarked that at this stage Germany had relatively few submarines in readiness; that she was not yet certain what novel counter-measures might be developed against them which would also be available to neutrals should they declare war; and that she was much concerned over losing important economic advantages arising from imports from the United States, which the British blockade had not then virtually cut off.

Consequently Germany's attitude was then largely one of fear as to the results of America's entering the war against her, and American protests were correspondingly effective.

By March of 1916, the German High Command had determined upon renewing the submarine campaign. The following reasons governing the decision are abstracted from the information furnished Admiral Scheer by the Chief of the Naval Staff:

> The general military situation is good . . . no serious danger is to be apprehended from America so long as our U-boats and Fleet remain afloat . . . from the economic point of view the fact that we are cut off from all imports from overseas and neutral countries becomes increasingly apparent . . . our opponents can hold out longer than we can. We must therefore aim at bringing the war to an end. . . . England can only be injured by war on her trade—a ruthless U-boat campaign—England will not be able to

withstand for more than six or eight months. Neutral shipping will also feel the full brunt of it . . . the small neutral states must give in and are willing to do so: that is, to stop trade with England. America opposes this manner of waging the U-boat campaign, and threatens us with war. From a military point of view, and especially from the standpoint of the Fleet, we might well risk this war. But economically it would fatally aggravate our situation . . . our aim, which is to bring the war to an end within a short time, would be farther than ever from realization, and Germany would be exposed to exhaustion . . . a break with America certainly affords us the tactical advantage of ruthless U-boat warfare against England, but only under conditions that will prolong the war, and will certainly bring neither relief nor amelioration to the economic situation.

In this second abortive submarine campaign the passenger steamer *Sussex* was torpedoed on March 24, 1916, with the loss of a number of American citizens. President [Woodrow] Wilson accordingly sent a very sharp note to the German government threatening to break off diplomatic relations, and the ruthless operations were promptly abandoned. Again the fear of military handicaps from the economic effects of America's becoming an enemy was conclusive in Germany's decision. No other consideration seems to have been a factor, and this is worthy of special note at this time when many Americans are seriously proposing removing all cause of future fear of us, as a means of keeping us out of war.

Following this second cessation of the submarine campaign in April of 1916, the Naval Staff made several unsuccessful efforts to have it resumed, and in September the question was again voted down at General Headquarters. On that occasion the principal governing reason was the military situation— the land campaign against Rumania then occupying the attention of an army whose services might be required against the Netherlands or other neutrals, should they be provoked into war by the submarine operations.

Once more, therefore, it was fear of military consequences alone, which protected neutral rights, and not until such fears were reasonably well dispelled was the final war on shipping decided upon. The fateful decision in favor of the ruthless submarine warfare that forced the United States into the World War was unquestionably predicated upon a firm German belief in our inability to defend our rights or to assist the Allied navies materially against U-boats. The latter craft were assumed to be virtually immune against naval attack, and hence able to prevent any great American troop movement overseas to the fields of France. As a matter of obvious logic and rationality, had the German High Command made the opposite assumption it would have reversed its conclusion and decision, our neutrality and rights would have been reasonably well respected, and America would not have been drawn into the war on this account.

In his *War Memoirs* General [Erich] Ludendorff outlines the proceedings of a special meeting at General Headquarters presided over by the Kaiser January 9, 1917, where the final submarine campaign was decided upon. After their then recent victories in Rumania the German troops so engaged were expected back on the home fronts before February 1, and there was therefore no longer any anxiety as to what Holland, Denmark, Switzerland, Sweden, or Norway might do. An American declaration of war, however, was recognized as practically certain. She would, no doubt, arm herself in the same way that England had done, but could not substantially increase her output of munitions that were already being supplied the Allies. In the first year she might put a maximum of five or six divisions of troops in France. Shipping deficiencies in consequence of submarining, however, would prevent transporting a greater force together with its supplies.

Neutral shipping would be frightened away from the war zone and add to the shortage resulting from the mounting submarine toll. This was carefully calculated to bring decisive results within six months despite all the anti-submarine efforts, which the Allies and America might make jointly. On these assumptions and recommendations of the Chief of the Naval Staff, Hindenburg favored the adoption of the submarine campaign. The Chancellor [Theodore von Bethmann-Holweg], who had previously opposed it on political grounds, now concluded [that] "the decision to embark on the campaign depends on the effects which are to be expected from it . . . if the military authorities regard it as essential, I am not in a position to withstand them . . . if success beckons we must act. Thus, was the Kaiser convinced and the momentous decision made."

A clear index of the German conviction at this period that America was incapable of effectively combating submarines is given by Ambassador [James W.] Gerard in *My Four Years in Germany*. Repeatedly questioned on this point he could only suggest that being a very inventive people we might devise some new weapon or method. Such a vague deterrent could scarcely influence an intention to begin a naval campaign which was fully expected to bring about decisive victory within six months. Even though the magical invention were made, much time would be necessary to apply it effectively on a big scale 3,000 miles overseas. Manifestly American naval impotence against submarines was a firm German assumption, and must have had a vital influence upon their final decision to embark on under-sea ruthlessness.

The Conversion of President Wilson

The weighty lesson carried in this massive load of national experience is manifestly that neutral rights can best be protected, without danger of war, through being well prepared for war. As George Washington put the same principle after his own experiences as President during the Napoleonic Wars and while Barbary Powers were also doing great harm to our sea-borne commerce:

> The most sincere neutrality is not a sufficient guard against the depredations of nations at war. To secure respect to a neutral flag requires a naval force, organized and ready to vindicate it from insult or aggression. This may even prevent the necessity of going to war.

The wisdom of Washington in this regard receives arresting endorsement from the fact that Woodrow Wilson, although starting out with an opposite opinion, finally reached the same conclusion as a direct result of similarly trying experience. Sincerely idealistic and pacific at heart, Wilson was shocked by the outbreak of the World War and promptly advised the nation to be scrupulously neutral in thought and act. He strongly and impatiently opposed further preparedness on our part, believing that it would be misconstrued by the belligerents and might even lead toward our participation in the great conflict.

The conversion of Wilson to Washington's viewpoint holds a profound lesson. Until late in 1915 he apparently clung to the conviction that moral suasion, held strictly apart from the threat of force, was the most certain means of maintaining neutral rights and avoiding war for us. His first public utterance indicating a change in this viewpoint was the speech of November 4th of that year before the Manhattan Club. Although the sinking of the *Arabic* in the preceding August had marked the end of the first ruthless submarine campaign as a result of our vigorous diplomatic protest, there were ominous signs of its renewal as soon as general circumstances were favorable to the Germans. It was becoming increasingly evident that moral suasion alone would not deter them permanently, and that the added influence of force was necessary.

We had also had serious differences with England, whose determined efforts to blockade Germany led to many costly detentions and seizures of American ships and to the gross expansion of the list of contraband. Although these practices were less goading than submarining (since innocent lives were not placed in jeopardy), they were illegal and indefensible, according to our State Department, and many Americans were deeply incensed over them and advocated war against Britain. The latter's unwillingness to heed our strong diplomatic protests was evidently another case of belligerent respect for neutral rights being contingent upon the influence of force. The policy of our government, according to Mr. [Robert] Lansing's *War Memoirs,* was not to allow such "controversies to reach a point where diplomatic correspondence gave place to action."

Viscount Grey [Edward Grey, 1st Viscount Grey of Fallodon] in his *Twenty-Five Years* reveals the corresponding British state of mind. "The Navy acted," he says, "and the Foreign Office had to find the argument to support the action; it was anxious work. British action provoked American argument; that was met by British counter-argument. British action preceded British argument; the risk was that action might follow American argument. In all this, Page's [the American ambassador in London] advice and suggestion were of the greatest value in warning us when to be careful or encouraging us when we could safely be firm." These general circumstances must have been known to President Wilson and to have further convinced him that the preservation of our neutral rights without recourse to war necessarily depended upon our having a navy sufficiently strong to give weight to diplomatic protests.

This was the background of Wilson's November 4, 1915, speech in which he reversed his previous position and strongly advocated increasing our armed forces: "not for attack in any quarter, not for aggression of any kind . . . but merely to make sure of our own security." He wanted "to be prepared not for war, but only for defense," believing that "the principles we hold most dear can be achieved . . . only in the kindly and wholesome atmosphere of peace, and not by the use of hostile force." He spoke "in terms of the deepest solemnity of the urgency and necessity of preparing ourselves to guard and protect the rights and privileges of our people. The Navy of the United States is already a very great and efficient force," he said, yet on the same occasion he advocated making it very substantially greater by beginning the largest naval building program ever undertaken, even to the present day. The Army was also to be materially strengthened.

President Wilson had obviously reached the conclusion as early as November, 1915, that if there was any way to keep out of the war while safeguarding our neutrality, it was through having amply strong armament with which to back our diplomacy. He was soon to receive stronger confirmation of this doctrine, and to realize the tragedy of having delayed preparedness until too late for it to be effective in any such way. Colonel [Edward M.] House was sent abroad in January of 1916, on a very important peace mission. Through him Wilson proposed a general conference to end the war. The Allies were first approached, with the assurance that should they accept and Germany reject, the United States would go into the war on their side. At first the proposal was received sympathetically but when in March Wilson insisted in qualifying our commitment by inserting the word "probably" the Allies refused the offer. Thus again, from another viewpoint, was the positive influence of force upon peace thrust upon Wilson's attention.

As previously stated, Germany renewed her submarine campaign in March of 1916, but in a few weeks once more abandoned it upon our virtual ultimatum threatening to sever diplomatic relations. Wilson among many other high officials seems then to have temporarily shared in the mistaken public assumption that moral suasion had again triumphed, whereas in fact the governing consideration was German fear of economic consequences. At this period the British also fanned our resentment against them by further restraints upon American trade, including the obnoxious "Black List" of neutral firms and persons with whom all trade was forbidden. The effect of these added provocations—both German and British—was to spur President Wilson to great heights in his advocacy of preparedness. Under his ardent sponsorship the huge naval building program was pressed through Congress and formally approved by him in August, 1916. He also toured the country making numerous extraordinary speeches calculated to turn public opinion strongly in favor of adequate armament.

The cause of preparedness has never received more impassioned, eloquent, logical, and convincing support than that given in 1916 by the previously pacifist minded President Wilson. Some of the strongest speeches were delivered in the winter and spring before his re-election, but all are worthy of the most careful study and consideration at this time when we debate the relationship between armaments, neutrality, and war. There is not the least doubt that as a result of his unequalled experience Wilson had become an ardent convert to the conviction that the preservation of just peace for us in a warring world required preponderant American armament with which to reinforce diplomacy. At St. Louis in February of 1916, he pleaded for "incomparably the most adequate navy in the world" for the United States, and he strongly supported such a doctrine even after the war was over, and until his death.

But the tragedy of Wilson's conversion is that it came too late, and that should be a fruitful lesson for the present generation. Ships appropriated for in August of 1916, could scarcely have had their keels laid by February 1917, when the Germans started their final submarine campaign. The forces, both military and naval, which Wilson advocated so earnestly during 1916 might well have forestalled the ruthless U-boats, and hence kept us out of war, had they been an effective reality at the time of the Kaiser's conference with the High Command in January, 1917. Certainly if we had then had sufficient means to quell submarines, the fateful decision would have been far different—and most likely reversed—and America no doubt would have remained at peace and at the same time enjoyed respect for her neutrality and vital interests.

The Examples of Other Wars

The prelude to our entry into the World War thus offers convincing argument for the need of adequate force as a means of keeping out of war while maintaining legitimate rights and interests unimpaired. Yet it is merely one among several chapters of American experience, which unmistakably point to precisely the same thing. Moreover in our entire history there are no examples which would lead to an opposite conclusion. Virtually all of our foreign wars possess the common aspect of having American non-preparedness, or assumed relative weakness, as a cardinal element in their origin. They thus point to military-naval strength as a general preserver of peace for the United States.

In the case of the Revolution a seafaring people were first aroused to resist the mother country by infringements upon their vital interests on the sea. The Colonies were totally unprepared for war, and had it been otherwise there can be little doubt that they would not have been provoked to the point of rebellion. Our Quasi-War with France (1798–1801) would not conceivably have occurred if the infant Republic had been able to give even moderate naval protection to its merchant vessels. The long continued and extensive depredations upon them took place while we were a neutral during a great war in Europe and when we had not a single man-of-war to safeguard our shipping. America's weakness then clearly invited the irksome violations of her neutrality and was hence a prime cause of her necessary resort to hostilities. Much the same were the circumstances which forced us to defend our interests and rights against Barbary piracy between 1801 and 1815, and in this instance we had even gone to the disgraceful length of vainly paying tribute to avoid war. Sufficient force from the first would have preserved our rights as well as our peace.

The genesis of the War of 1812 is better known. In principle it closely paralleled that of our part in the World War. Two strong belligerents in Europe exasperated us beyond endurance by illegal and gravely injurious practices against our commerce on the sea, which the American navy was too weak to protect adequately. In 1812 we had as just a complaint on this score against France as against England, and finally chose the latter as an antagonist because of her added provocation respecting impressment. Our relatively negligible naval power at this period commanded no respect against the aggressive violation of neutrality that forced us into the fruitless war.

America's only other foreign wars of any considerable magnitude were those with Mexico in 1846 and with Spain in 1898. Neither one fits the condition of a general war in Europe under which it is now being alleged by many American idealists that disarmament would favor preserving our neutrality and keeping us at peace. Nevertheless, both of these relatively small wars serve to illustrate the war hazard that is inherent in naval weakness. Our occupation of Texas in 1846 that brought on the clash of arms was precipitated by British and French diplomatic maneuvers aiming at control of Texas. These European countries would scarcely have entertained such intentions had the power of our Navy commanded their respect. In the case of the war with Spain in 1898, although America's navy proved itself under test to be substantially superior, this was a great surprise to European authorities who had freely predicted the reverse. In advance of hostilities Spanish statesmen felt confident of naval victory. Otherwise they would have been more careful to keep peace with us by reasonable concessions respecting Cuba.

The circumstances leading up to our various foreign wars therefore offer powerful arguments in favor of preparedness as a means of avoiding war, especially so under the condition of a great conflict abroad in which our neutral rights are jeopardized. In these instances a lack of sufficient force as an ally to diplomacy was usually a prime factor in the provocation, which left us little choice but the use of arms. The opposite side of the same case, the influence of adequate force to keep peace and maintain our interests, has also been well demonstrated on many occasions in history. Among American experiences of this nature the most illuminating is the French evacuation of Mexico after the Civil War in consequence of our vigorous diplomatic demands, although numerous other lesser incidents could be cited.

Conclusion

Reviewing all the factual evidence that is available—the historical experiences set forth herein and much more for which there has not been space—the conclusion is inescapable that preparedness is the most certain way to keep out of war, and is the only way in which we can do so while maintaining just and essential interests. The apostles of the opposite thesis of "Peace Through Disarmament of America in an Armed World" can present only the illusory logic of academic idealism. Such persons are necessarily far more dangerous guides than Washington and Wilson—idealists of the first magnitude and statesmen of great eminence, whose opinions were matured by potent experience in high office and in the crucible of grave responsibility.

And moreover, all other American statesmen, with scarcely any exception, have come to the same general conclusions whenever experience under responsibility in such matters has served them. Wilson's eloquent advocacy of "incomparably the most adequate navy in the world" was mainly predicated in his mind upon the maintenance of our neutrality with justice and peace. He pleaded for this nearly eighteen months before we were drawn into the war, largely from want of such a force. And after the Armistice he went forward vigorously with the building of such a navy despite very active foreign diplomatic opposition. He wanted then to be certain of preserving the peace and justice that victory had won. Grueling experience had taught him the same lesson for today that Washington had learned in the same hard school, more than a century before: "the most sincere neutrality is not a sufficient guard against the depredations of nations at war." For this a powerful naval force is indispensable and "may even prevent the necessity of going to war." No greater wisdom is available for our guidance now as we look forward to the ominous prospect abroad.

SIX

A Special Relationship

Roosevelt encouraged Knox to engage in a missionary quest to educate the American public about the role of the U.S. Navy in both peace and war. Between 1934 and 1941, Roosevelt consulted with Knox to successfully establish basic foundations for future leaders to continue pursuing their maritime vision of the United States. Invoking the Monroe Doctrine and the maritime tradition of "freedom of the seas," Roosevelt implemented a strategy designed to avoid direct American involvement in foreign wars. On these grounds, the president justified a grand maritime alliance with the British Empire after 1937. The sinking of USS *Panay* (PR 5) in Chinese waters further inspired Roosevelt to pursue a strategy of collaboration between the Royal Navy and U.S. Navy—pooling maritime resources to defend common global interests, contain mutual enemies, and ultimately avoid wars ashore.

Roosevelt included Knox in strategic discussions intended to navigate the difficult nexus between peace and war. Roosevelt also expanded negotiations between the Admiralty and the Navy Department. In examining the Roosevelt plan to establish a transatlantic naval alliance, Knox advised that the "British conception of 'national defense' is much broader than ours." "They fight with rates of exchange, loans, mercantile shipping, commercial treaties," he continued, "all correlated with international politics, military and naval action."[1] Following the advice of Knox, among others inside the Navy Department, Roosevelt offered to recognize the "Greater East Asian Co-Prosperity Sphere" of Imperial Japan in order to shift U.S. Navy forces from the Pacific to the

Atlantic during the summer of 1941. Focusing on common international rivals, Roosevelt entertained a maritime alliance between the British Empire and United States. At the same time, he did not support the imperial system and remained wary of British intentions.

Given the inherent dissimilarities within the governmental and military establishments of the British Empire and United States, transatlantic collaboration evolved slowly. Bureaucratic problems and petty politics further hindered Roosevelt in his efforts to frame maritime strategy. The operations and intelligence subdivisions remained completely dysfunctional within the departments of State, War, and Navy. As a result, information concerning potential military threats failed to reach the appropriate levels of strategic command—as U.S. Navy warships shifted from the Pacific to engage in a quasi-war in the Atlantic. To implement his maritime strategy with greater efficiency, Roosevelt acted upon recommendations from Knox to consolidate authority under the CNO and reestablish geographic fleet headquarters in the Pacific, Atlantic, and Asian waters.

Efforts to influence global affairs with sea power remained in an unfinished state of development as Roosevelt struggled to avoid war. Ultimately, the Imperial Japanese Navy achieved complete surprise by demonstrating the novel tactic of employing aircraft carriers on a long-range strike against the U.S. Navy anchorage at Pearl Harbor. The tragedy of 7 December 1941 transformed American maritime strategy and remained a persistent influence on the military policy of the United States. During the Second World War, Roosevelt reluctantly presided over the militarization of American society. He also hoped to develop a reconstruction strategy designed to demobilize the United States while preserving global order under the "four policemen": Great Britain, the Soviet Union, the Republic of China, and the United States.[2]

Within the informal context of maritime history discussions, Roosevelt solicited advice from Knox in formulating a grand maritime strategy centering on the transatlantic alliance between the British Empire and United States. During the Second World War, Roosevelt continued to encourage Knox in his efforts to rally American voters to embrace the Navy as a symbol of pride and national prestige. From shipyards in the Midwest to those on the coasts, American industry thrived in support of the wartime Navy. Roosevelt and Knox directly participated in the rapid expansion of the fleet, from fewer than 380 warships in 1938 to a reported 6,768 by 1945, and Roosevelt envisioned a persistent peacetime mission for the Navy. War veterans also gained an appreciation for the sea, whether their service featured extended time in Navy warships or they spent time in troopships en route to the global warfronts.

Roosevelt and Knox perceived an opportunity to recast popular memories of the Second World War to emphasize the Allied victory at sea. Roosevelt encouraged Knox to emphasize this message in planning a "national" museum of the Navy. Since the early 1930s, with Congress providing initial funding for the project, Roosevelt and Knox had shared the dream of constructing the museum off the National Mall in Washington, D.C. They planned to place the historic warships USS *Constitution,* USS *Constellation,* USS *Hartford,* and USS *Olympia* on permanent display on the shores of the Potomac River, along with an adjacent museum holding artifacts and imagery of the Navy. Although the idea ultimately died with Roosevelt in 1945, Knox continued nurturing their shared dream through the Naval Historical Foundation.

In a previously unpublished narrative, Knox described his special relationship with Roosevelt. Neither embraced the idea of a standing American military presence on land after the Second World War. At the same time, both recognized a standing peacetime function for the Navy: to continue operations in support of a new global order under the United Nations. This mission did not necessarily require the application of violent force. Derived from historical studies of maritime affairs, it was intended to frame a future concept of American sea power to attain strategic "influence" and avoid future conflicts altogether.

ASSOCIATION WITH FRANKLIN D. ROOSEVELT

PREVIOUSLY UNPUBLISHED MANUSCRIPT, 1948

Prepared at the Request of the Franklin D. Roosevelt Memorial Foundation

Until his becoming President, my association with Franklin D. Roosevelt was quite casual and only occasional. I saw him when he was Assistant Secretary of the Navy several times on very minor official matters, and again socially at receptions at his residence. Then, as always, he and Mrs. Roosevelt were both exceptionally gracious and charming.

He was no longer in office upon my assuming charge of the Office of Naval Records and Library in 1921. Among my new duties was custody of the Navy Department's precious collection of old manuscript records, dating back to the Revolution. Upon moving the collection several years later one of the bound-up volumes appeared to be missing. Inquiry was made of a number of persons, whose habits of research suggested the possibility of their furnishing a clue. Among these was the ex-Assistant Secretary [Roosevelt]. He replied promptly and of course deploring the loss. Incidentally, he mentioned the great physical affliction that had recently come upon him, of which I had been unaware. The missing volume was found later, but I neglected so to inform him.

I witnessed his being sworn in for the first time as President and heard his stirring inaugural address with great admiration; especially the memorable phrase, "the only thing we have to fear is fear itself."

Some weeks after the inauguration, to my great surprise he sent for me. About seven years had passed since our exchange of letters over the missing volume, but instantly he inquired about it. I replied it had been found, and he seemed much relieved.

The special purpose of the summons, however, was to give me (for the library) his personal set of printed official documents dealing with naval affairs in the period during which he had been Assistant Secretary of the Navy. Although we had the set already, the value and interest of his copies were enhanced by their bearing his signature, which as a collector himself he of course well knew. His act was thus one of unique generosity and considerateness, more especially so coming in the midst of the trying national crisis confronting him. During nearly an hour I was cross examined on the affairs of the office, and he proposed that to serve historical ends some of the old manuscript records should be printed, which met with my enthusiastic response. I was charged with drawing up a general plan.

At a subsequent conference he approved the plan of first publishing naval documents pertaining to our quasi-war with France (1798–1801). This was to be followed similarly by the Barbary Wars, the War of 1812, and the Mexican War. Meanwhile, the assembly of badly scattered source material on naval affairs in the Revolution was to be proceeded with, and publication undertaken when done. Thus, all wars up to the Civil War would be covered and the naval documents dealing with that war had been already printed.

In the case of the Civil War documents the publication (thirty volumes) had been wholly at government expense and the books given away. For the now projected earlier wars the President proposed that the government bear the costs of production, but that it be reimbursed by sale of the volumes to the public at cost. He arranged for passage of the Act of Congress that authorized the project on that basis. My part was to engineer the matter into the budget, prepare material for the Public Printer, and keep the President generally informed, especially as to difficulties needing his aid in overcoming them. At one Budget hearing a traditionally "hard boiled" Budget official [Daniel W. Bell] cross-examined me in detail on the project for half an hour, making written notes of my replies. At the end, he smiled and said he wanted the specific information because he had "orders from the White House to give Dudley Knox all he asked for." Thereafter, matters went smoothly, with only an occasional need for his help, which was promptly forthcoming when I sent him a brief note.

An essential preliminary to publication of the French War documents was the location and copying of a substantial quantity that were scattered in private hands—principally in eastern libraries and historical societies. Years before, the President himself had collected a considerable number, as well as naval documents pertaining to other early wars also. He generously consented to our free use of his large collection, for the copying and publication of any items chosen. To this end I went to Hyde Park in the summer of 1934 and was most graciously met by him in the large reception room. He preferred to give personal attention to the matter because of his intimate familiarity with his own collection.

On a large table near the fireplace the collection was piled nearly two feet high, arranged by groups in bulky manila envelopes. He went through the lot, one by one, calling my attention to enclosed items that might be of interest but leaving the selection entirely to me. This went on nearly an hour, with interludes of discussion on the project, respecting which he made general and very pertinent suggestions freely. I called out nearly 100 documents dealing with the French and Barbary Wars as being suitable for copying. To my surprise he handed them to me with off-hand instructions to take them along. Not even a list of them was made. Most collectors are miserly and at least would have delicately suggested a receipt!

It seemed appropriate that the president should sign a foreword to the first volume of the projected great series, and he readily consented to doing so. Such a procedure would also be very helpful in making the project self-liquidating, in the government's interest. Accordingly, I formulated a forward which he signed after editing it. When the first volume came off the press I brought a copy and took it to him, requesting that he autograph it. Instead of then and there signing, he laid the volume aside, after examining it with great interest and obvious satisfaction, saying he would return it in a few days. Duly it came to me with the following in his own hand:

> *For Dudley Knox—in appreciation of*
> *a dream of yours and mine come true—*
> *Franklin D. Roosevelt*

During the course of his Presidency a series of seven volumes of documents on the "Quasi-War with France" were printed, and also a similar series of seven volumes covering the "Barbary Wars." Since the project proved to be only about fifty percent self-liquidating, Congress became increasingly less inclined to appropriate the necessary funds and finally stopped them altogether, upon completion of the Barbary Wars series near the beginning of our entry into the Second World War.

Naval Pictures

The President's special love of naval prints and paintings is well known. At irregular intervals he would refer matters of identity to me. The first occasion of this was a few months after his assuming office, when he asked me to the White House to look at two prints he contemplated buying.

About five years previously a gentleman from a remote section of Virginia had unexpectedly mailed me two colored prints depicting phases of our naval attack against Tripoli (1803–04). They were in tight rolls and torn here and there, so that laying them out flat involved risk of further tearing. The gentleman asked $25 dollars each for them. I was then unversed in prints and their value. However, the scenes were new to me and I offered to have the prints repaired and laid flat on backing if he would allow me to photograph them for the naval records; he to accept the risk of further damage in the process. All this was done and the repaired prints returned.

These were the prints which found their way to the President's hands in 1933. Upon my arrival at his desk he greeted me with one hand and rang a bell with the other. In walked a secretary [Grace Tully] most carefully carrying a large flat package done up in white tissue, that was gently laid on the desk. The President gingerly opened the wrapping and said, "have you ever seen these before?" He was surprised and amused when I answered "yes" and told him the story.

But more to the point, for the collector, was, had I ever seen any others like them? No, I had not, and I believed them to be rare. Moreover, I was beginning to realize from greater experience that I had been foolish not to buy them in the first instance. The President said the asking price was now $100 dollars apiece and that he had offered $75. At what amount he finally purchased them I do not know, but they soon became two of the rarest items in his unique collection of naval prints.

After a few years the Corcoran Gallery held a special exhibit of that print collection, together with the President's naval paintings and ship models. No catalog had ever been made and Mr. [Cuthbert Powell] Minnegerode, Director of the Gallery, wanted one for the exhibit. The President nominated me for the job and I was happy to do.

During the course of the exhibit the President very kindly gave me permission to photograph the entire collection for the pictorial files of the Navy Department. Our photographer, [Petty Officer First Class John] McCarthy, a splendid young enlisted man, worked at this diligently and enthusiastically. His camera was mounted on a tripod on the slippery floor. One day a leg slipped and the camera fell upon a glass case covering a ship-model. Case and model were both overturned and the masts and spars of the model rather badly broken. Much greater damage was done to poor McCarthy's feelings, and my own! However, our apprehensions were proved to be unwarranted by the President's typically generous reactions. He was unperturbed by the bad news as to his precious model and quite content over the subsequent repairs that were made.

Interest in Naval History

The President's interest in and knowledge of naval history was exceptional. On one occasion, Judge [Samuel Irving] Rosenman sent for me to check on the accuracy of some matter that the President had inserted from memory in the draft of a forthcoming speech. It was an important speech on foreign policy, and by way of illustrating the need of protecting our maritime interests the President drew upon our experiences in the Barbary Wars. His insertion from memory had been absolutely accurate.

Similarly his recollection of the minor details of early naval history was most unusual. This was borne out by his frequent reference to them in ordinary conversation. One of this had an amusing side. His naval Aide, Admiral Wilson Brown, burst into my office one morning quite breathless having hurried over from the White House. Without preliminaries he said, "do you know who Moses Brown was?" "Yes," I replied, "he commanded a small man-of-war in the Quasi-War with France. I have recently received a photograph of his portrait, send by a descendant." Pointedly, Brown asked "do you see any resemblance to me" and implied some Jewish possibility.

Showing him the photograph it was clear that Moses Brown was a gentile, and I inquired the reason for his questions. He had made the usual routine morning call on the President. The latter was busily occupied with papers on his desk, and upon glancing up had said, "hello Moses Brown." Puzzled, the Admiral replied, "did you say '*Moses*,' Mr. President?" "Yes," came the answer "I did say '*Moses*;' don't you know who Moses Brown was?" The aide had to acknowledge his complete ignorance whereupon the President said, "you go over and ask Dudley Knox."

The President's special interest in naval history was conspicuously illustrated by the publication of a Mexican War sketch book in water colors; made originally by the sloop-of-war *Dale* in California and Pacific Mexican waters during hostilities with our southern neighbor a century ago.

The President had the book on his desk at the White House when I arrived in response to a message in 1938. The folio volume contained nearly thirty full-page watercolors of battles and naval scenes. Although "primitives," the art work was exceedingly good. As sources of naval history the pictures were of exceptional interest because of the great scarcity of contemporary materials, especially sketches but even including written documents. It was just the sort of item that a discriminating connoisseur would have eagerly acquired. The President said that it had come to his attention about twenty-five years previously in a small antique shop in the countryside of Pennsylvania, and he had then bought it. I expressed great interest in the book, stressing its historical value.

He had sent for me because "some friends" of his had persuaded him to publish it in colors. But such a work would require rather copious text, not merely to explain the meaning of each picture but also to give them all a proper setting within the framework of a general narrative. Would I do the text? I would, very gladly. "But," said the President, "you should receive some compensation." I replied that that was entirely unnecessary; it would be very interesting work, and I would be glad to undertake it without any compensation. He was insistent that I should have about $200. Equally firm that the matter of compensation was superfluous, I walked out with the book, the debated issue remaining undecided.

In a few days, Mr. Bennett Cerf, of Random House, communicated with me to arrange publication. This was a protracted matter. The color plates were made in Meriden, Connecticut, whereas the printing of text and the binding was done in San Francisco. Of the special type used there was an insufficient quantity available for complete printing in one step. Mr. Cerf had arranged with the President that the latter write an introduction, which was considered as essential to the best success of the book. The President was much preoccupied with the critical state of affairs in Europe, while World War II was in its early stages. Consequently, I made a preliminary draft of an introduction which he altered but little.

The writing of the narrative for the series of pictures proved to be unusually interesting. More especially was this true because the sketches themselves bear convincing testimony that the conquest of California was an almost wholly naval achievement—afloat and ashore—contrary to the generally accepted version which assumes far too much relative credit to the Army.

Upon submission of my manuscript text to Mr. Cerf, I was very much surprised to receive a check for $400. I had no financial arrangement whatever with him, and the amount was twice that which the President had mentioned to me as appropriate—and which I had maintained was unnecessary. Obviously, entirely without my knowledge the President had bargained for me with Mr. Cerf, and moreover had doubled the amount which he intimated to me might be a fair compensation. I have always regarded the incident as an interesting example of the President's great generosity of spirit.

The publishers also very kindly sent me two copies of the product of all this; the superbly handsome limited edition of *Naval Sketches of the War in California*. One copy I took to the President, asking him to autograph it. After a few days it was returned to me with the following inscription in his handwriting on the fly-leaf:

Thanks to my old friend Captain
Dudley W. Knox, U.S.N. These old
sketches have been made to live again.

Franklin D. Roosevelt
The White House
October 30, 1939

Thus was it transformed into a cherished heirloom for my grandchildren.

That the genius of Franklin D. Roosevelt was many-sided is commonly recognized. Whatever may have been the measure of his knowledge and proficiency in other lines there can be no doubt as to American naval history. In that field, he had few if any peers.

[signed]
Dudley W. Knox
September, 1948.

SEVEN

Root Problems in
Joint Doctrine

K nox held a position of influence that far exceeded his
bureaucratic station at the Navy Department. Serving in
uniform with a retired rank of Navy captain, he helped
negotiate the grand maritime alliance between the British Empire
and United States during the Second World War. President Roosevelt and Admiral King consulted with Knox in advance of meetings with the British. In this role, Knox drew from his special
understanding of the British military organization to adapt equivalent American bureaucracies for the purposes of wartime collaboration. Among other projects, Knox examined the functions
of the British Joint Chiefs organization to facilitate transatlantic
collaboration in 1940.[1] Building upon Knox's recommendations,
Roosevelt established the Joint Chiefs of Staff (JCS) by *temporary*
executive order in 1942. Under the unified command of the JCS,
American military and naval commanders synthesized operations
on an unprecedented global scale.

The British Empire centered on unified civil-military organizations with strategic headquarters based in London, which extended
to regional commands ranging from Bombay to Singapore and
Hong Kong. Under the War Cabinet, the Joint Chiefs in London
reported to the prime minister. The Joint Chiefs were comprised
of the three ranking representatives of the British army, air force,
and navy. The organization set London at the center of worldwide
operations, a placement that ultimately proved difficult to coordinate as Imperial Japanese forces struck in Asia, popular revolts
threatened British control in the greater Middle East, and German

and Italian forces advanced in continental Europe and North Africa. The British Empire teetered on the brink of collapse and Churchill asked Roosevelt for assistance from the United States.

Following the attack on Pearl Harbor, the British pressed their American counterparts to reorganize for the purposes of transatlantic wartime collaboration. As the British drew from centuries of experience, the Americans recalibrated their bureaucracies to fit within a combined transatlantic alliance. The reorganization process remained in a state of constant renovation within the American government, punctuated by frequent congressional accusations leveled against the Roosevelt administration for overstepping the wartime emergency limits of executive authority. Among other extraordinary wartime measures, Churchill and Roosevelt created the Combined Chiefs of Staff (CCS) to bring the senior levels of both nations together in January 1942. Shortly thereafter, the British Joint Chiefs formally established the "Joint Staff" mission to represent British military interests in Washington and to serve as the liaison to the American JCS. However, British observers also noted differences between the British joint staff organization and the American analogue as established under the JCS. Additionally, the wartime JCS suffered under awkward personality dynamics, which shaped relations between the services and served as a catalyst for changes after the war.

In writings published between the world wars, Knox directly participated in the competition between the War Department and Navy Department. The U.S. Army questioned the role of the U.S. Marine Corps, and Navy aviators fought Army counterparts on theories of strategic airpower, precision bombing, and tactical ground-support missions. These unresolved debates carried into the wartime deliberations of the JCS, which originally included the CNO, Adm. Harold R. Stark, and the CominCh, Adm. Ernest J. King, chief of staff of Army general George C. Marshall. As special advisor to Roosevelt, Adm. William D. Leahy served in retired status to act in an informal intermediary role on the JCS.[2] When Stark sailed for London to become ComNavEu in April 1942, King wanted to install the commandant of the Marine Corps, Lt. Gen. Thomas Holcomb, on the JCS. Seeking a more equitable balance, Marshall insisted upon the appointment of U.S. Army Air Force general Henry "Hap" Arnold.

Under emergency wartime executive powers, Roosevelt empowered the JCS to circumvent the traditional authorities of the civilian secretaries of war and navy. British models of "combined" and "joint" military organization further influenced changes in American civil-military organization. Although members of the JCS remained subordinate to the civilian secretaries of war and navy, the Joint Chiefs held unique access to the wartime White House. British representatives in Washington criticized the American JCS as an organization that lacked cohesion, suffered from ambiguous legislative authority, and often struggled to overcome traditional service rivalries.[3] In large measure, the wartime success of the JCS ultimately centered on the personalities of Marshall and King.[4] Although they often disagreed, the two officers ably represented their individual services by presenting a united front during the CCS's Anglo-American negotiations.

Anticipating the Allied victory in the Second World War, Knox advised King in preparing the Navy's strategy for reorienting the service for peacetime operations. The two men followed the Navy philosophy of creating organizations for functions of finite scope and duration, seeking means to avoid bureaucratic duplication and entrenchment. Within this context, the concept of unification remained an underlying theme in the relationship between the War Department and Navy Department. Knox worked with King in articulating the Navy's plans for the postwar era, saying that "there is perhaps a popular misconception that the Army and Navy were intermingled in a standard form of joint operational organization." King emphasized that "there can be no hard and fast rule for setting up commands in the field." He advised Secretary of the Navy James V. Forrestal, "It is my earnest conviction, whatever else may have been learned as to the most effective relationship of the ground, naval and air forces, the most definite and most important lesson is that to attempt unity of command in Washington is ill-advised in concept and would be impracticable of realization."[5] Fearing the prospect of being inextricably tied to the British system, Knox agreed with King in recommending the dissolution of the JCS and other wartime bureaucracies.

Knox examined the inherent problems of organization, which coincided with the steady demise of the British Empire and the new role of the United States in global affairs. In doing so, he addressed the problems of "unification," which remained a persistent theme in debates concerning the question of "joint" doctrine through the Cold War era and beyond. In the following essay, "The Development of Unification," Knox provided a very sharp critique of the military policy of the United States. He revisited familiar themes to put forth the U.S. Navy's argument that sea power furnished the means to safeguard peaceful commerce and avoid future wars. He challenged the European concept of strategic airpower by emphasizing American traditions, which placed the civilian commander in chief in firm control over both an army and navy. On the question of airpower, Knox disagreed with the establishment of a separate U.S. Air Force and reasserted the importance of land-based tactical aviation forces for Army operations ashore and sea-based aircraft aboard Navy warships.

Building upon the firm grounds of American civil-military tradition, Knox offered a strong argument against the postwar trend toward bureaucratic centralization within the American defense establishment. He warned against the functional approach, which emphasized technological curiosities to justify efforts designed to unify American airpower, communications, and intelligence. Among other factors, Knox worried about the notions of a "special relationship" and an "iron curtain" as articulated by Churchill in a March 1946 speech delivered at Westminster College in Fulton, Missouri.

Knox worried that British models of civil-military organization progressively served as a basis for American policymakers to introduce fundamental changes within the government of the United States. Within this context, Knox once again offered a potent justification for maintaining the American traditions of a separate War Department and Navy Department. As the strategic functions performed by the land and sea services remained focused on the uniquely different environments ashore and at sea, both the Army and Navy required the capacity to harness aviation, communications, and intelligence.

In the essay, Knox drew from his unique understanding of the problems inherent in the British model of centralized civil-military bureaucracies and referred to American historical traditions to question the underlying logic of unification. He identified key problems in the efforts surrounding the development of the centralized Department of Defense, Central Intelligence Agency (CIA), Armed Forces Security Agency (AFSA), U.S. Air Force, and Armed Forces Staff College. He directly refuted the rationale employed to justify abandonment of American traditions in order to create new organizations, perceptively identifying the problems Congress had consistently revisited since 1947. In recent times, those problems have been addressed through the Goldwater-Nichols Act of 1986 and the 9/11 Commission Report of 2004. Today there is again a call to look at the organization of our national security apparatus to search for efficiencies and more effective ways to defend the nation. The arguments Knox offered in the following essay resonate amid persistent debates concerning American concepts of civil-military organization, especially within the context of foreign alliances, combined operations in peacetime, and the problems of ambiguously framed "joint" doctrine.

THE DEVELOPMENT OF UNIFICATION

1950

The House Armed Services Committee has done a most constructive national service in pointing the way towards sound development of unification. Its report on the controversial investigation that it made last year on aviation matters is filled with wise comment and valuable suggestions for future guidance that the armed services will do well to digest and follow.

With fine perspicuity the Committee concluded that service prides, jealousies and rivalries had "only a bare minimum of influence on this controversy," and pointed to "fundamental professional disagreements on the art of warfare" as the root cause. This view is fully in accord with [Naval] War College teaching that a commonly held "conception of war" within a military organization is all but indispensable. When leaders think differently of the ways in which war should be conducted, inevitably sand enters the machinery of cooperation. Under such adverse conditions it matters very little what the outward forms of organization and administration may be. Until the intangibles of conviction are well resolved there can be no genuine unification. It can only be a deceptive sham, a theory without sufficient substance to make it effective in defending the country and in supporting national policies.

A cardinal problem that now confronts us in the development of true unification lies in the chasm separating Army and Navy concepts of organization, administration, and operations. Let us remember that these have evolved from widely differing conditions and experience through nearly two centuries. Habits and customs established in such a way have a psychological fixation that cannot be substantially changed overnight. They correspond to what psychologists call "mores" of personal character, akin to instinct. Such ingrained attitudes necessarily require considerable time and new experience before lasting alteration of them can be effected. We of the Navy accept as a matter of course that a ship must be even more than a unified organization. We know beyond the least question that she has to be closely integrated internally, with coordination achieved through the authority of a single individual. Otherwise she cannot be effective enough as a unit in combat or other emergency. In principle the same pattern applies to fleets and to naval shore stations. Perhaps from long association with the Navy, the Marine Corps is also more than a unified body. It also is closely integrated, including all of its various elements—even its aviation. Within both the Navy and the Marine corps, integration amounts to an instinct.

This has never been true of the American Army. Since its origin seventeen decades ago it has never been truly unified—much less integrated. In reality it has been a loosely knit aggregation of semi-independent Corps, rather than an Army. Traditionally Cavalry, Infantry, Artillery, and Quartermaster Corps come to mind, each almost a separate empire. In recent years the first three have been merged at top levels, but custom seems still to keep them unintegrated lower down. Then we have Corps of Engineers, Inspectors, Judge Advocates and others, each largely sufficient unto itself. As Armies grew in size and land warfare increased in complexity, the strong tendency was to create additional, semi-autonomous Corps. Recent decades have seen the Artillery and Quartermasters each split into two separate corps, and new ones established such as Signal, Ordnance, Chemical, Finance, Tank, and Air.

All this represents a basic difference between Army and Navy organizational administrative concepts in the very period when some of the foregoing Army Corps were born the Navy abolished its Engineer Corps and Construction Corps and integrated their functions with the Line. To the Army a new element in warfare suggests a new Corps. Its trend towards dis-unification has ever been strong, and in sharp contrast to the naval and the Marine Corps impulse towards integration of each new element into the general body.

The great divergence of these two viewpoints was never more pronounced than in the case of aviation. Its advent reacted upon the Army as a reason for adding one more to its already numerous aggregation of Corps. As aviation grew rapidly into a major element of combat, the Air Corps expanded correspondingly not only in size but also in independence. Finally the centrifugal force of this rapid movement flew the Air Corps entirely out of the Army's orbit. The re-named "Air Force" became completely independent of the Army—and this in the name of "unification," to the complete mystification of the Navy. A sailor could be forgiven in believing that the most logical first step towards unification of the Armed Services would have been the unification of the loosely-knit Corps-ridden Army itself; including the actual integration of Air Corps with Army rather than separation of the two.

It is a paradox that the cardinal cause of separating Air Corps from Army—the primary combat importance of aviation—was the very reason influencing the Navy to integrate aviation within itself ever more intimately. In unity there is strength. The closer the integration of ships and planes the more powerful is their joint effort. Sea-air power as a merged entity is a much stronger oceanic combination than if divided into two semi-independent elements of ship-power and plane-power.

A great wealth of war experience has so amply proved the soundness of this concept of naval power as to make it incontestable. The successes of the integrated American and Japanese Navies proved it, as did the reverses of the British and other navies while they were un-integrated. This accounts for the volcanic eruption of naval feeling and resistance to the recurring efforts towards transferring naval aviation, or any of its legitimate naval functions, to the control of land aviation authorities. To the Navy such separation would be a fatal operation, like dissecting out of the human body its circulatory system, or several vital organs. This view is diametrically opposite to the Army's supine concurrence in lopping off its Air Corps, as though it were an unessential protuberance.

Here then is a fundamental difference in concepts of war that calls urgently for reconciliation among the Armed Services if they are to recognize the wisdom of the House Committee and be guided by it rationally. The principles underlying integration of aviation with naval surface forces seem equally applicable and compelling for land armies. Our Marine Corps has set a standard unmatched by any other American military organization. It is unique in having its own aviation closely integrated with ground combat units. The splendid effectiveness of this true unification was superbly demonstrated in many contests of the late war and since then in Korea. Recent ill-considered suggestions to abolish the Corps must have been in blissful ignorance that the art of close-in aviation support of ground troops would thereby have been lost in this country—quite aside from losing leadership in amphibious warfare as well as destroying the best example we have of esprit and morale. Parenthetically it may be observed that morale can be built up and sustained more readily in relatively small organizations and that consequently the unification of them into large groups, when carried too far, tends to lower the standard of morale.

There is one basic and indispensable requirement for true unification or integration of aviation with surface forces, whether afloat or ashore. The aviators must have sufficient competence in surface warfare (on sea or land) to comprehend the effect of their efforts from aloft upon the course of operations below. However good a pilot may be as a flyer, and however good his plane and weapons, he cannot support surface forces well without understanding how they fight and their combat problems. By the same token surface commanders must be well enough versed in aviation to understand its needs, difficulties, capacities, etc. Otherwise the two arms cannot possibly work together as a well-coordinated team, nor can the full value of air support be realized.

This dual, basic requirement is the rock which from the start has split apart and hurled in opposite directions the thinking of Navy and Marines on the one hand, and Army and Air Force on the other hand. The separation of the Air Corps from its Army followed principally from ignoring this requirement. Here, then, is another concept of war which the Armed Services must harmonize if their unification is ever to be a reality rather than mere theory. In a recent article in *Foreign Affairs* Admiral [Charles M.] Cooke has stated the case clearly. He says that since 1920 "a naval aviator was a qualified naval officer, and naval officers, many of them aviators, became increasingly indoctrinated in aviation. Naval Officers were air minded, and, no less important, air officers were surface minded; without this general understanding of naval principles, and experience and proficiency in surface operation, the air officer could not understand the possibilities of his own arm." Nor could the surface officer possibly appreciate the tremendous potentialities of a genuinely integrated "air-surface" force. The whole set-up very naturally led to the development of an aviation component of sea power.

With the Army it was quite different. The several Line Corps took little interest in the potent new arm that was developing under their noses. The flyers of the Air Corps nearly all lacked proficiency and training as soldiers. Even General [William] Mitchell, the principal early leader, had been first commissioned from civil life into the Signal Corps and never had considerable military line experience. Almost automatically this whole background led the Air Corps to develop aviation as something quite apart from the Army proper, and ultimately, actually to separate from it. The Corps' main interest usually lay in independent action, principally strategic bombing.

Because of the consequent neglect of the function of close tactical air support to ground troops, the potency of which was amply demonstrated by the Germans and Russians in the late war, Admiral Cooke now argues that "soldiers need wings." He contends that "years will be required to create an experienced body of ground indoctrinated air personnel, and air-indoctrinated ground personnel, and to develop special equipment and methods. This growth will be accompanied by continuously changing tactical concepts, and even changes in strategic concepts, to fit in with the increased mobility and offensive power that our ground-air force will acquire." He also feels that "the integration of our ground forces . . . with an expanding ground-air element, is today the most pressing task of our military leaders." I agree fully.

II

A number of other seriously conflicting concepts of warfare need to be reconciled if the Committee's advice is to be taken seriously and the national interest well served. Among these is the question of overseas air bases. For some years the Air Force has contended that the increasing radius of action of planes diminishes the need of advanced bases, and even the need of navies. We now have planes capable of taking off from the United States, bombing Russia and returning home non-stop. Then why should distant overseas air bases be necessary or desirable? Within this question lies another—the justification of the large carrier, which in essence is an air base of great mobility.

The principles involved were clearly illustrated by the great B-29 strategic bombing of Japan during the late war. Taking off from Tinian-Saipan, these giant planes had the radius to bomb Japan and return non-stop to base, which they did do for some months. But the land aviation leaders urged that the halfway island of Iwo Jima was needed also, as an intermediate air base, and accordingly the Marines with naval support took it in a major operation. The losses were heavy; what was the gain? First, the B-29s could be given fighter protection over Japan, substantially reducing their losses and enabling them to bomb more effectively from lower altitudes. Second, damaged B-29s could be saved from loss by using Iwo as an emergency landing place. Additional to these two advantages was a third of even greater importance, which alone tripled the effectiveness of the entire enterprise through tripling bomb loads. General [Henry H.] Arnold explained the matter in this way:

when the field or fields have been constructed, making staging operations possible . . . take-off from the Saipan and Tinian bases, flight to target (Japan) and return to Iwo Jima for fuel will permit a B-29 to carry 16,000 pounds of bombs on high altitude missions, as against the 6,000 pounds of bombs now carried. For flight from (Saipan-Tinian) base to Iwo Jima, refuel and flight to target and back to base (Saipan-Tinian) will permit 20,000 pounds of bombs to be carried.[*]

Had the tiny island been big enough to serve the whole force as a refueling point on both the outward and return flights, then bomb loads could have been six times greater than was possible when operating from Saipan-Tinian alone.

How profoundly significant all this is! Bomb power could be multiplied by six merely by moving the forward base half way to [the] target. Each plane could fly more missions within a given time. More damaged planes could be saved because of the shorter return to base. Fewer planes sustained damage because of the protection afforded by fighters, with the new base within fighter range. The effectiveness of bombs dropped was perhaps doubled from the greater accuracy at the lower altitudes permitted by fighter protection. All in all, combining the several factors, it would seem ultra-conservative to conclude in principle that total effectiveness over the target can be multiplied by ten when the distance of the forward base from the target is cut in half.

Naturally, this holds true only when long distances are involved. And further qualifications are in order for varying conditions of the problem, such as different types of planes, types of bombs, etc. Nevertheless the principle is thoroughly sound that by advancing take-off bases closer to the target the power of aviation attack on the target may be greatly multiplied. This is the general concept of the Navy and Marine Corps. To them the contrary view of the Air Force that the long range plane eliminates the advisability of intermediate and forward bases in trans-ocean work seems very fallacious, since such elimination necessarily takes a heavy toll in reduced power over the target for all types of planes and weapons.

Intimately associated with this question of overseas air bases is that of finance. The apportionment of the defense dollar among the three services is involved; also the matter of how much drain is put upon the national resources

---

[*]Henry H. Arnold, *Report of the Commanding General of the Army Air Forces to the Secretary of War—Third Report* (Washington, D.C.: Government Printing Office, 1945).

for the total defense budget. Once upon a time the alleged cheapness of air power was advanced as a big reason for its development in place of sea power. That fallacy is rapidly becoming apparent. There may be room for argument on the basis of first cost alone, but that is far from the whole story. When we build a ship she lasts as a useful wartime unit for upwards of 30 years. Airplanes on the other hand are much less durable physically, and moreover become obsolete much more rapidly. One should multiply the first cost of airplanes by four or five to reach a true comparison with the first cost of ships.

The several hundred B-36s already built or on order stand the defense budget at upwards of $2 billion dollars for first cost over a period of but a very few years. According to press reports they are being rapidly outmoded by the development of a new type of plane, which presumably will require another initial outlay of about $2 billion. But these sums are apparently only a starter. Within the last few weeks the press has announced that our air forces have now reached the level which will require two billion dollars annually to maintain, principally because of normal necessary conversions and replacements due to wear and obsolescence.

It would seem that a reasonable degree of frugality is becoming rather imperative, all the more so if it can be done without diminishing our bombing strength over the target. This combination would be extremely difficult without adopting a general concept of necessarily utilizing advanced air bases. By such adoption very great savings could be made. We have seen in analysis of the Iwo Jima case that moving a base forward by half the distance to target multiplies bombing effectiveness by nearly ten. In reverse terms, this is equivalent to saying that for the same result at the target, in principle one plane based on the forward half-way point will do the work of ten planes operating only from the rear base.

The same principle is quite applicable to our trans-Atlantic strategy. The Air Force thesis of basing on continental America for non-stop bombing of Russia and return, simply means ten times more planes employed in the enterprise than would be necessary, for the same target effect, if a forward half-way base were used. Of course the same principle can be applied a second time, by halving the distance to target once more, with a corresponding further gain superimposed on the first. Since ten times ten equals one hundred the theoretical extreme might be that one plane operating from a second advanced base could equal the effect over the target of one hundred planes restricted only to a base in the United States.

Although such a "100 to 1 shot" appears rather fantastic, yet it is sound in theory. Rather than go so far, a compromise would seem sensible. Let us assume that we had two advanced bases, one half-way between home and target, and the second advanced to three quarters of that total distance. If then we cut the bombing force ten times, it might still exert ten times more power at the target than could the original force operating solely from the United States.

The foregoing is put forward as a conception of bombing warfare, in conjunction with the utilization of advanced air bases, as a means either of greatly increasing power at the target or the saving of large sums of money, or both. But the naval forces necessary to establish and protect bases are also very expensive. On balance would bases more than pay their way financially? We have already pointed out that ships are four or five times more durable than planes, with a corresponding factor in their favor on the first cost comparison. Many other factors enter into such a problem which would require very complicated calculations to solve. On the whole the author is thoroughly convinced that overseas bases will much more than justify their utilization on a cost basis, considering the reductions they make possible in the numbers of exceedingly expensive planes.

But it is unnecessary to argue the matter under existing circumstances. As a legacy from the war, we have a huge fleet in mothballs that will be available for twenty years at least, for any needful naval effort in connection with the wartime establishment and protection of overseas air bases. Naval first costs in such operations would be negligible, compared with the many billions earmarked or projected for planes greatly in excess of the number required if bases are properly utilized.

A fair question would be, where could suitable bases be located that would satisfy the theoretical conditions set forth above? Assuming a bombing campaign against Russia, a wealth of positions might become available, depending in each case upon the political attitude of the countries having sovereignty over them.

III

Closely related to the matter of overseas air bases is that of the carrier. The heated controversy over the projected carrier USS *United States* (CVA-58) appears to have arisen from two causes: (1) Sharply differing concepts of war between the Navy and Air Force, largely as to the utility of overseas air bases, and (2) apportionment of the defense dollar.

Aside from the carrier's great value in many other kinds of naval operations it would necessarily be a key unit in the establishment, protection, and supply of overseas air bases; especially so in the early stages of such an enterprise. In fact, without carriers the establishment and adequate support of trans-ocean air bases would be an impossibility in many cases where severe resistance in the air, on the ground, or at sea was encountered.

The carrier is itself primarily an air base; a unique one of exceptional value as such. In certain unfriendly quarters much emphasis has been placed upon the alleged vulnerability of carriers, particularly to attack by land based aircraft. The late war clearly demonstrated the exaggerations in this, and indicated that the palm for vulnerability to air attack goes decidedly to land air bases, in comparison with carriers. These ships are very hard to hit from the air, especially so for pilots of land planes who are seldom proficient when their target is moving at high speed. This was proved many times over in the late war. Then again, modern techniques of protecting carriers by an umbrella of fighters besides numerous attending vessels carrying extremely heavy anti-air batteries, confronts attacking planes with a veritable inferno of resistance. Few survive if they venture close enough to hit, while those maintaining relatively safe distances seldom harm a fast moving target. Of course, carriers are not immune to damage from the air. A cardinal predicate of warfare is that losses are involved. But land air bases are more vulnerable to damage than are carriers. The land base has to stay put whereas in addition to its other defensive advantages the carrier can move away from a hot spot.

A highly mobile air base is an especially potent instrument of offense. It can strike heavily with great surprise, from unexpected quarters and at unexpected times, and then withdraw at will from counterstrokes. The fixed land base has nothing comparable to this. But perhaps the most unique and valuable attribute of the carrier is its uncanny ability to apply the principle of multiplying the value of air power, by moving the launching point of planes rapidly towards the target.

In previous sections, this principle has been explained, dwelt upon, and illustrated by citing the case of Iwo Jima. It was shown that for long distance work, by merely advancing an air base half way to the target, bombing power over the target is automatically multiplied by from six to ten. This is equivalent to multiplying the number of planes by such a factor. The first step can be repeated and the multiplier squared, and even perhaps cubed. Consider now the carrier advancing on her prey and rapidly multiplying the power of her planes automatically with every turn of her propellers. There is no such magic in land air bases, nor in the planes operating from them.

These and other carrier concepts require clarification in many minds (if one can judge by the opposition in various quarters) to the end that more genuine unification of thinking among the Armed Services may be achieved.

We are fortunate indeed that the House Committee in its invaluable report on Unification and Strategy should recognize the utility of giant carriers, and stand forthrightly for naval guidance to the nation in such technical naval affairs.

In these days of guided missiles, jet propulsion, atomic power and a great variety of other new weapons and devices we cannot, of course, rely too precisely upon recent wartime experience for future guidance. Nevertheless the steppingstones of all forms of genuine human progress are laid in foundations of the past. It is normally true that firm advances rest upon well proven principles which only require altered forms of application to them of what is new.

CONCLUSION

Fighting for History

As a Navy man, Knox initially took an applied approach to history by seeking lessons from past wars. He eventually developed a deeper understanding of history, recognizing that the factors that influenced past conflicts could never be replicated for direct application in future battles. Drawing from a unique command of history, Knox ultimately influenced the naval policies of four presidential administrations. He helped envision a Navy second to none before the First World War and then had a key role in drafting the legislation required to create a two-ocean Navy in anticipation of the Second World War. The combined fleets of the Royal Navy and U.S. Navy unified to establish irrefutable command of the seas. By 1945, the Anglo-American alliance was transforming global affairs, although the transatlantic balance largely shifted from London to Washington during the world wars. The British Empire remained the underlying foundation upon which the American vision of a United Nations evolved in the aftermath of the Second World War. Within this postwar context, Knox continued working behind the scenes to frame an American strategy for the peacetime reconstruction and a new global order.

Longstanding personal ties with President Roosevelt and Admiral King provided inroads for Knox to gain unique influence in framing strategic concepts of sea power and American maritime history. Through service in two world wars and then in his published work, he also contributed to the critical discussions that resonate in contemporary debates concerning the future military policy of the United States. Having participated in the unification debates, King and Knox lamented the death of Roosevelt, worried about the decisions of President Harry S. Truman, and feared the potential consequences of American involvement in foreign entanglements.

Without Roosevelt at the helm of American policy, King and Knox attempted to set the bureaucratic foundations for the Navy to navigate the uncharted waters of a new global strategic mission for the United States. As both approached age seventy by 1945, King and Knox continued working with a new generation of war-seasoned Navy leaders to remember the traditional *peacetime* role of American sea power, as exemplified in the naval genius of George Washington, the quasi-wars of American maritime history, and the basic tenets of the Monroe Doctrine, which shaped Roosevelt's strategy leading up to the Second World War.

After receiving a lifetime appointment with five-star rank as a fleet admiral, King rewarded his shipmate, confidant, and mentor. Among his last acts as the CNO, King nominated Knox for promotion to the one-star rank of commodore on the active list of the Navy. Under this amplified authority, Knox continued nurturing the bureaucratic ties between the Naval War College, ONI, and ONH during the Second World War and beyond. He formally retired with a one-star commodore's rank in 1946, with more than fifty years before the mast. In retirement he continued working as a civilian at ONH, where his co-workers all referred to him as "Commodore." History remained at the center of his life as Knox embarked on a new postwar mission, helping to shape American strategy through the postwar reconstruction and into the unsettling realities of the Cold War era.

History emerged as a key element in the Navy strategy to facilitate reconstruction in Europe and Asia. In his role as director at ONH, Knox continued supervising the unprecedented effort to reconstruct, analyze, and preserve German historical records. Between 1945 and 1949, Knox supervised the collaborative efforts of ONI and ONH to microfilm the German naval archives. Fusing intelligence gathering with historical research interests, his organization successfully translated in excess of 30,000 pages of captured German documents to create the Tambach Collection, which also contained a complete duplication of the original records within an estimated 4,391 reels of microfilm.[1]

Initially housed within the secure vaults of ONI, the Tambach Collection was eventually transferred to ONH for historical research purposes. Knox helped efforts to declassify the collection for use by historians.[2] In particular, he facilitated the research of the collection's semiofficial historians, Rear Adm. Samuel Eliot Morison, USNR, and Harvard University professor Robert G. Albion. Characterizing the historical significance of the Tambach Collection, Morison observed that until "German Admiralty records were examined . . . almost everyone in the United States and Great Britain thought that the submarine campaign had been prepared long in advance." From reviewing German records, Morison discovered that "nothing could be further from the truth."[3]

The interrelationship between historical research and naval strategy remained a central theme in global American policy. Knox played a key role in preserving historical records of past American wars. He also framed historic preservation efforts within the context of American strategic interests after the Second World War. For example, Knox served as an advisor to the former CNO, Chester W. Nimitz, to facilitate improved relations with the Japanese during the 1950s. As the honorary chairman of the Naval Historical Foundation, Nimitz pioneered the American fundraising campaign to salvage and restore the predreadnaught warship *Mikasa*, the historical flagship of Admiral Tōgō at the Battle of Tsushima. Having fallen into complete disrepair, the rusted hulk of *Mikasa* reflected the demise of Japan as a maritime power after 1945. Coinciding with Anglo-American strategic efforts to shape affairs in Asiatic waters during the Cold War era, Knox assisted Nimitz in marshaling Naval Historical Foundation resources to help restore *Mikasa* in 1953. Eight years later, the U.S. Navy also provided assistance to install *Mikasa* on static display near the naval base in Yokosuka. The historic warship marked the renewed prominence of Japan as a regional naval power.[4]

Knox and the Naval Historical Foundation operated on the fringes of interservice competition to shape the future military policy of the United States. Knox continued in an informal naval advisory role when Adm. Louis Denfeld relieved Nimitz as CNO. At this time, in a valedictory speech delivered in 1947, Nimitz delivered a strong argument against the concept of creating a separate U.S. Air Force. As the new CNO, Denfeld continued to push the naval policies of his predecessors and ultimately ran afoul of President Harry S. Truman for criticizing the decision to establish a separate U.S. Air Force. The panacea of unified command ran against basic naval traditions, which placed less importance on centralized headquarters ashore in order to encourage a unified effort among forces deployed farther from home.

Denfeld warned the Truman administration about the problems of unification, formally articulating his concerns in testimony to Congress. Centralization in aviation, intelligence, and communications further eroded Navy influence with the creation of the U.S. Air Force, Central Intelligence Agency, and Armed Forces Security Agency. Knox also advised Denfeld as the Navy navigated the difficult waters of unification. Both earnestly feared the prospect of such organizations blossoming into vast and uncontrollable bureaucracies. Knox preferred a more traditional approach in efforts to develop an American strategy, emphasizing the basic foundation of the Monroe Doctrine and the policies envisioned by the late Franklin D. Roosevelt. He feared the bureaucratic consolidation of American military and naval power as the services fought for airpower.

Unification changed the traditional character of civil-military relations in the military policy of the United States. The secretary of the navy, James V. Forrestal, fought against the establishment of the Department of Defense and criticized the decision to create the CIA and AFSA. With reservations, Forrestal reluctantly accepted the appointment to serve as the nation's first secretary of defense in 1947. Facing dwindling budgets, Denfeld engaged in an unofficial public affairs campaign to undermine the basic premise of a separate air force and directed the assistant CNO for guided missiles, Rear Adm. Daniel V. Gallery Jr., to draft the infamous "Gallery Memorandum." This classified point paper was leaked to the public when journalist Drew Pearson published excerpts in the October 1949 installment of his nationally syndicated column, "Washington Merry-Go-Round." The controversy surrounding the question of airpower and the atomic bomb ultimately demoralized Forrestal to the point of mental exhaustion, and he resigned his post in the spring of 1949. His successor as secretary of defense, Louis Johnson, forced the CNO, Denfeld, to resign, further adding to the tensions among the services.[5] The tumultuous circumstances surrounding the removal of Denfeld as CNO also contributed to the depressed mental state of Forrestal, and in November he committed suicide.

The tragic circumstances surrounding the Forrestal suicide amplified the controversy among the American military services. In the wake of Forrestal's death, Knox and his son, Dudley Jr., asked Gallery to soften his insubordinate tone, which appeared under titles like "The Admiral Talks Back to the Airmen," "Don't Let Them Sink the Navy," and "If This Be Treason." Gallery proudly recalled in one letter to Knox that "the boys who wore the lighter shade of blue were mighty miffed when they heard that I referred to them as the 'Air Farce' in a speech—the term spread quickly beyond my control."[6]

Knox encouraged efforts to highlight the wartime successes of the Navy, which served as an indirect means of countering the Air Force in public affairs. During the war, Gallery had earned a heroic reputation for capturing the German submarine U-505 in June 1944. Knox had assisted the Navy public affairs campaign at the time, which portrayed Gallery as a figure comparable to the mythologized naval heroes Horatio Nelson and John Paul Jones. The junior Dudley S. Knox had also served under Gallery during the U-505 capture, and Knox took great pride in his son, who returned from the war with a Navy

Cross and continued serving in the U.S. Navy Reserve. The junior Dudley S. Knox used GI bill funding to complete a law degree, help fellow veterans to secure postwar benefits, and assist his father as a legal advisor with the Naval Historical Foundation, Naval Order of the United States, and Navy League.

The Gallery and the Knox families collaborated in efforts to preserve *U-505* as an American naval war memorial in Chicago, although the idea of placing a "Nazi" submarine on display as an *American* war memorial seemed odd for many in the public.[7] In the 30 August 1953 edition of the *Chicago Sun-Times,* an article highlighted the effort to "Raise $44,000 in Drive to Bring Nazi Sub Here." Knox helped counter such critiques and recast the image of the *U-505* as a symbol of American naval commitment, editing the speech delivered by Fleet Admiral William Halsey Jr. "Here today we have spectacular proof that the spirit of John Paul Jones and his sailors of our early days, still lives in the modern Navy of today," Halsey observed. *U-505* "should be a stern warning to the communists that we believe in our way of life, want no part of theirs, and we are willing and capable of defending our way."[8]

Knox assisted Gallery in equating the historical imagery of German submarines with the potential threat of Soviet submarines. By invoking the familiar U-boat menace of the world wars, they helped justify reinvestment in Navy antisubmarine forces during the Cold War. In retelling the heroic story of the U-boat's capture in various articles and in the memoirs *Clear the Decks* and *Twenty Million Tons under the Sea,* Gallery creatively overstated the importance of Navy aviation by crediting his pilots for the capture of *U-505*. Such tales proved too much for the junior Dudley S. Knox, who had actually facilitated the capture as skipper of the destroyer escort *Chatelain*. The junior Knox dutifully reported to Gallery that on

> page 216 of your book [*Clear the Decks*], it was brought home to me that the general public at large, and many naval officers could easily assume that the fighter pilots brought the *Chatelain* over to the submarine almost single handed. Knowing you as I do, I came to the conclusion that an error, or some misconception of the facts existed in the official documents covering this incident. . . . It is obviously incorrect to conclude that the *U-505* capture was one of "the few cases in which an aircraft actually directed the attack." . . . I am therefore sending a copy of this letter to the Director of Naval History, with the request that it be placed in the official files of the Department, as a supplement to my original report on the capture of U-*505*, dated 8 June 1944.[9]

In the end, Knox placed higher priority on telling the truth in recounting historical events. He shared his son's letter with Rear Adm. Samuel Eliot Morison, who inserted a footnote in volume 10 of the semiofficial *History of United States Naval Operations in World War II*. Morison warned readers that "*Clear the Decks!* chap. X gives additional details about the towing, but is somewhat inaccurate about the capture."[10] In the postwar effort to refute the concept of a separate U.S. Air Force, Knox agreed with Gallery on the importance of highlighting the role of naval aviators in retelling heroic accounts of Navy operations during the Second World War. However, Knox also emphasized the importance of historical objectivity by using documentary evidence to reconstruct facts as accurately as possible. In examining the events culminating in the capture of *U-505*, Morison avoided weighing in on the account provided by Gallery and the younger Knox. Rather, Morison left it to the reader to consider both perspectives.

Influence, Sea Power, and History

Knox crafted a compelling vision of the U.S. Navy, a vision that continued to evolve beyond his lifetime. Inspired by the proud traditions of the Royal Navy before the First World War, he played an instrumental role in preparing the U.S. Navy for victory after the Second World War. In examining the rise of the U.S. Navy in global affairs, the influence of Knox appears within the subtext of Henry L. Stimson's recollections of service within the War Department and State Department. In a memoir published in 1947, Stimson recalled the "peculiar psychology of the Navy Department, which frequently retired from the realm of logic into a dim religious world in which Neptune was God, Mahan his prophet, and the United States Navy the only true church."[11] In spite of Stimson's partisan perspective in recounting his experiences as secretary of war, he acknowledged the firm foundations upon which the Navy had become an unbeatable force of American sea power. Building on the teachings of Mahan and others, Knox and his generation of American naval professionals directly influenced the culture of the service through two world wars and into the Cold War era.

Service traditions and history have remained crucial influences upon American sea power and Navy operations in both peace and war. In 1966, six years after Knox's death, the Navy Department formally acknowledged his central role in creating a Navy second to none: his son was an honorary sponsor for the keel-laying ceremonies surrounding the construction of an entirely new class of destroyer, with the first of that class christened as the USS *Dudley*

W. Knox (DD 1062). The choice to name a destroyer after Knox was fitting. Given his early career in torpedo boats and surface warships, he had helped to develop the traditions of the contemporary Navy destroyer fleet. Unfortunately Dudley S. Knox passed away before the warship launched. However, Knox's granddaughter, Janet Knox Sturtevant, presided at the ship's commissioning ceremonies in 1969. Carrying forward the family traditions, his other granddaughter, Tina Knox Radigan, represented the family at the ship's decommissioning.

Knox set an example for contemporary Navy professionals who seek insight from history to conceptualize the future influence of sea power on the military policy of the United States. Indeed, Knox's name is featured prominently at the Naval Postgraduate School in Monterey, California. The Naval War College Archive and Library also holds documents and books that Knox and his associate, Tracy Barrett Kittredge, assembled in the 1920s and 1930s. This material remains available for students who wish to pursue a deeper understanding of the historical role of maritime strategy in achieving a sustainable peace. In 2013 the Naval Historical Foundation also established a commemorative medal for maritime historians with the Dudley W. Knox Naval History Lifetime Achievement Award.

Studying this sampling of essays, readers can see that Knox covered a wide spectrum of themes and historical subjects, all of which hold lasting resonance. This collection loosely revisits three main themes—influence, sea power, and history—which Knox consistently addressed in published works, lectures, and within the cloistered ranks of the Navy. Throughout the service's history, naval professionals have continually revisited questions of strategy, leadership, and operational doctrine. The fundamental influence of history on concepts of sea power also served as an underlying current within Knox's essays. Warning about "vanishing traditions," he rallied readers, encouraging them to embrace their role as caretakers of historical materials, to draw perspective from the past, and to recognize the trends that define the nexus between peace and war.

Knox understood the guiding influence of history on contemporary problems of American strategy and global maritime policy. For this reasons, leaders like Roosevelt and King solicited advice from Knox during the unprecedented period of change in the first fifty years of the twentieth century. Often working behind the scenes, Knox shaped pivotal decisions during both world wars through personal associations with American presidents, generals, and admirals. He disliked the political infighting that often defined affairs within the halls of government, although he celebrated the American system of checks and balances. Invoking idealized examples from American history, he provided full-throated justification for maintaining naval forces in peacetime. Navies provided a means to *avoid* war through diplomacy, he argued. Should diplomacy fail, naval forces could be employed decisively—often without having to commit American ground forces on extended adventures to foreign shores.

With the passage of time, the writings of Knox faded into obscurity. Contemporary readers may question the value of preserving traditions, perhaps even challenging the relevance of history. But in this respect, Knox continued in the custom of Mahan, who recognized the inherent relevance of history to the Navy—the importance of understanding contemporary concepts of sea power and the influence of the past on future strategic challenges. Knowledge of these elements is important to the ongoing dialogue about the proper role of the United States in global affairs. In works published during the first fifty years of the twentieth century, Knox examined naval trends and offered pertinent opinions about the role of the Navy, American sea power, and the stabilizing influence of the United States. His opinions continue to carry weight into the twenty-first century.

NOTES

Introduction: Below the Surface of Naval History

1. Dudley W. Knox, "The Navy and Public Indoctrination," Rough Notes and Article Drafts, Box 13, Dudley Wright Knox Papers, Library of Congress, Washington, D.C. (hereafter cited as Knox Papers).

2. Peter Karsten, *Naval Aristocracy: The Golden Age of Annapolis and the Rise of American Navalism* (Annapolis: Naval Institute Press, 2008); Ronald Spector, *Professors of War: The Naval War College and the Development of the Naval Profession* (Newport, R.I.: Naval War College Press, 1977), 72–87, 100–10, and 117–28; Robert O'Connell, *Sacred Vessels: The Cult of the Battleship and the Rise of the U.S. Navy* (New York: Oxford University Press, 1993), 302–22.

3. Alfred Thayer Mahan, *Influence of Sea Power upon History, 1660–1783* (Boston: Little Brown, 1892), 11.

4. Dudley W. Knox, "Naval Power as a Preserver of Neutrality and Peace," Box 13, Knox Papers.

5. Ernest J. King and Walter Muir Whitehill, *Fleet Admiral King: A Naval Record* (New York: W. W. Norton, 1952), 81 and 148.

6. Roy C. Smith, "Discussion of 'The Role of Doctrine in Naval Warfare,'" U.S. Naval Institute *Proceedings* 41, no. 2 (March–April 1915): 362.

7. King and Whitehill, *Fleet Admiral King*, 74.

8. "Memorandum of conversation with Commodore D. W. Knox, 31 May 1946," Folder 5, Box 5, Ernest J. King Papers, Naval Historical Collection, Newport, R.I. (hereafter cited as King Papers).

9. King and Whitehill, *Fleet Admiral King*, 74.

10. "ASW Conference 1 March 1943 Remarks by Admiral King," keynote address by King, prepared on 28 February 1943, Walter M. Whitehill and Thomas Buell, comps., Folder 5, Box 7, King Papers.

11. "Memorandum of conversation with Commodore D. W. Knox, 31 May 1946."

12. King and Whitehill, *Fleet Admiral King*, 74.

13. *Hearings before the Subcommittee of the Committee on Naval Affairs of the United States Senate*, 66th Cong., 2nd sess. (Washington, D.C.: Government Printing Office, 1920), vol. 1, p. 727.

14. King and Whitehill, *Fleet Admiral King*, 106.
15. Dudley W. Knox, "The Role of Doctrine in Naval Warfare," U.S. Naval Institute *Proceedings* 41, no. 2 (March–April 1915): 330.
16. Knox, "Navy and Public Indoctrination."
17. Dudley W. Knox, "Our Vanishing History and Traditions," U.S. Naval Institute *Proceedings* 52, no. 1 (January 1926): 15.
18. Knox, "Navy and Public Indoctrination."
19. Andrew Lambert, *The Foundations of Naval History: John Knox Laughton, the Royal Navy, and the Historical Profession* (London: Chatham, 1998), 30, 121–22, and 231–32.
20. *Hearings before the Subcommittee of the Committee on Naval Affairs*, 1–9 and 253.
21. Dudley W. Knox, Ernest J. King, and William S. Pye, comp., "Report and Recommendations of a Board Appointed by the Bureau of Navigation Regarding the Instruction and Training of Line Officers," U.S. Naval Institute *Proceedings* 46, no. 210 (August 1920): 1265–93.
22. Oral History of Ambassador Alan Goodrich Kirk, 182, microfilm from the Columbia University Oral History Office, John T. Mason, ed., Manuscript Collection, Naval Historical Collection, Newport, R.I.
23. "Dyer interview of 1 August 1945," p. 5, Manuscript Register Series Number 22, comp. Evelyn Cherpack, Folder 7, Box 7, King Papers.
24. William S. Sims, *The Victory at Sea* (New York: Doubleday, Page, 1920), 243.
25. Churchill to Sims, 31 March 1919, Box 51, William S. Sims Papers, Library of Congress, Washington, D.C.
26. Knox, King, and Pye, "Report and Recommendations of a Board," 1273.
27. Ibid.
28. Edward C. Kalbfus, comp., *Sound Military Decision* (Newport, R.I.: Naval War College Press, 1936), 42–45.
29. *Command and Employment of Air Power*, Field Manual 100-20, Field Service Regulations, War Department (Washington, D.C.: Government Printing Office, 1926), 1.
30. Dudley W. Knox, *The Eclipse of American Sea Power* (New York: American Army and Navy Journal, 1922), 121.
31. Dudley W. Knox, *The Naval Genius of George Washington* (Boston: Houghton Mifflin, 1932), 5.
32. Sarah M. Goldberger, "Challenging the Interest and Reverence of All Americans: Preservation and the Yorktown National Battlefield," in *Destination Dixie: Tourism and Southern History*, ed. Karen L. Cox (Gainesville: University Press of Florida, 2012), 185–203.
33. Knox, "Navy and Public Indoctrination."
34. Knox, "Preserver of Neutrality and Peace."

35. "Association with Roosevelt," September 1948, 7, Box 24, Knox Papers. The full title of the volume is *Naval Documents Related to the Quasi-War between the United States and France.*
36. Knox, "Preserver of Neutrality and Peace."
37. "Nimitz Gray Book," Chester W. Nimitz Papers, U.S. Naval War College, Newport, R.I., online at https://www.usnwc.edu/Academics/Library/Naval-Historical-Collection.aspx#items/show/849, accessed 5 January 2015.
38. Administrative Histories of the Second World War, Naval History and Heritage Command (hereafter cited as NHHC), Library Branch, Washington, D.C., comprises three hundred bound volumes and supporting texts, organized by specified administrative subdivisions, fleet commands, and shore establishments. More specifically, readers are encouraged to examine the volumes by Elting E. Morison examining the office of CNO, that of Walter Muir Whitehill on the commander in chief, U.S. Navy, that of James A. Michener on the major command's "Numbered Fleets," and that of Tracy Barrett Kittredge on the ComNavEu Headquarters.
39. "Naval History of the Current War," 31 July 1944, Folder 12, Box 48, Records of the Commander in Chief, U.S. Navy (CominCh) and Chief of Naval Operations, Record Group (RG) 38, Naval Archives and Records Administration (NARA).
40. "Microfilming Archives in Enemy Countries," memorandum from Lt. Cdr. Peter van der Poel to Kittredge, 4 August 1943, serial A-12 (9), "Axis Archives," Folder 53, Box 10, ComNavEu, RG 313, NARA.

Chapter One: Marching to the Sound of Guns

From U.S. Naval Institute *Proceedings* 39, no. 1 (March 1913): 41–62
  1. See the U.S. Naval Institute *Proceedings* issues from 1914, which include the essays by Dudley W. Knox, "The Great Lesson from Nelson for Today" (March–April): 295–318 and "Old Principles and Modern Applications" (July–August): 1009–39.
  2. Knox, "Great Lesson from Nelson," 295.

Chapter Two: Historical Foundations for Adaptation

From U.S. Naval Institute *Proceedings* 41, no. 2 (March–April 1915): 325–54

Chapter Three: The Ethos of American Naval Command

From U.S. Naval Institute *Proceedings* 46, no. 12 (December 1920): 1883–1902
  1. George C. Dyer, *The Amphibians Came to Conquer: The Story of Admiral Richmond Kelly Turner* (Washington, D.C.: Naval Historical Center, 1972), 123–24.

2. J. E. Jenks, ed., "Politics in Navy Administration," *Army and Navy Register* 68, no. 2085 (3 July 1920): 6.

3. Knox, King, and Pye, "Report and Recommendations of a Board," 1273.

4. Ernest J. King, "A Wrinkle or Two in Handling Men," U.S. Naval Institute *Proceedings* 49, no. 3 (March 1923): 427–34.

Chapter Four: Forgetting the Lessons of History

From U.S. Naval Institute *Proceedings* 52, no. 1 (January 1926): 15–25

1. Knox, King, and Pye, "Report and Recommendations of a Board," 1273.

2. Entry for 5 January 1923, Thomas C. Hart Personal Diary, 1914–1960, photocopy, Papers of Thomas C. Hart, NHHC. Special thanks to Professor John B. Hattendorf for calling my attention to this reference.

Chapter Five: The Navy as Peacemaker

From U.S. Naval Institute *Proceedings* 63, no. 5 (May 1937): 619–26

1. D. W. Bell to FDR, 12 February 1935, Box 24, Knox Papers.

2. D. W. Bell to FDR, 24 February 1935, Box 24 Knox Papers.

3. James Brown Scott to Knox, 15 January 1937, pp. 1–3, Box 24, Knox Papers.

4. "Reviews and correspondence, 1935–1942," Folders Relating to Manuscript *A History of the United States Navy,* Speech, Article, and Book File, Box 19, Knox Papers.

5. Dudley W. Knox, "Naval Power as a Preserver of Neutrality and Peace," rough draft, Box 13, Knox Papers.

Chapter Six: A Special Relationship

1. Memorandum for Adm. Harold R. Stark, 6 January 1940, Box 24, Knox Papers.

2. David Roll, *The Hopkins Touch: Harry Hopkins and the Forging of the Alliance to Defeat Hitler* (New York: Oxford, 2013), 178 and 320.

Chapter Seven: Root Problems in Joint Doctrine

From U.S. Naval Institute *Proceedings* 76, no. 12 (December 1950): 1308–15

1. Memorandum on British Organization of National Defense, 6 January 1940, Box 24, Knox Papers.

2. "JCS Organization," Folder 25, Box 7, King Papers.

3. "History of British Admiralty Delegation to the U.S.A.," 12–18 and 280–81, Admiralty 199/1236, British National Archives, London.

4. Mark A. Stoler, *Allies and Adversaries: The Joint Chiefs of Staff, the Grand Alliance, and U.S. Strategy in World War II* (Chapel Hill: University of North Carolina, 2006), 2–22, 145–58, and 103–22.

5. Ernest J. King, ed., *The U.S. Navy at War: Official Reports to the Secretary of the Navy by Fleet Admiral Ernest J. King, U.S. Navy* (Washington, D.C.: Navy Department, 1946), 172.

Conclusion: Fighting for History

1. "Memorandum for Intelligence Officer, Microfilming Facilities, Survey of," 28 May 1945, 3–6, ComNavEu Axis Archives, ComNavEu, RG 313, NARA.
2. "Microfilm Copies of Records of the German Navy, 1850–1945," RG 242.8, NARA.
3. Samuel Eliot Morison, *History of United States Naval Operations in World War II: The Atlantic Battle Won, May 1943–May 1945,* vol. 1 (Boston: Little Brown, 1956), 4.
4. Duncan Redford, ed., *Maritime History and Identity: The Sea and Culture in the Modern World* (New York: Palgrave, 2013), 51–60.
5. Jeffrey G. Barlow, *Revolt of the Admirals: The Fight for Naval Aviation, 1945–1950* (Washington, D.C.: Naval Historical Center, 1994), 137–41.
6. Gallery to Knox, 15 September 1953, Folder 6, Archival Documents and Correspondence, U-505 Collection (U-505), Collections Department Archives, Museum of Science and Industry, Chicago.
7. David Kohnen, "Tombstone of Victory: Tracking the U-505 from German Commerce Raider to American War Memorial, 1944–1954," *Journal of America's Military Past* (Winter 2007): 1–25.
8. Halsey dedication address, 25 September 1954, OP-57 File, Box 38, Daniel V. Gallery Jr. Papers, Special Collections, Nimitz Memorial Library and Archives, U.S. Naval Academy, Annapolis.
9. Dudley S. Knox to Gallery, 21 January 1953, 1–3, Addendum to Report of 8 June 1944, Chatelain, Enclosure A, 2, TG.22.3, Records of the Commander in Chief, U.S. Navy and Chief of Naval Operations, Action Reports, RG 38, NARA.
10. Ibid., 1–3; Samuel Eliot Morison, *History of United States Naval Operations in World War II: The Atlantic Battle Won, May 1943–May 1945,* vol. 10 (Boston: Little Brown, 1956), 290. The emphasis on naval aviation and personal opinions offered by Gallery ran squarely against the political agenda and defense appropriations priorities favored by the ranking civilian policy makers in the Pentagon.
11. Henry L. Stimson and McGeorge Bundy, *On Active Service in Peace and War* (New York: Harper, 1947), 506.

SELECTED WORKS BY KNOX

"The Abortive Duel on Hicacal Point." U.S. Naval Institute *Proceedings* 74, no. 9 (September 1948).

"The 'Adams' Men-of-War." U.S. Naval Institute *Proceedings* 58, no. 11 (November 1932).

An Adequate Merchant Marine as an Auxiliary to the Navy and Army in Time of National Emergency. New York: Gardner Press, 1933.

"An Adventure in Diplomacy." U.S. Naval Institute *Proceedings* 52, no. 2 (February 1926).

"Another Side of the 5–5–3 Argument." *Scientific American,* August 1925.

"'Column' as a Battle Formation." U.S. Naval Institute *Proceedings* 39, no. 3 (September 1913).

"D'Estaing's Fleet Revealed." U.S. Naval Institute *Proceedings* 61, no. 2 (February 1935).

"Defense of United States Naval Policy." *Current History Monthly* 22 (June 1925).

"Development of Unification." U.S. Naval Institute *Proceedings* 76, no. 12 (December 1950).

"The Disturbing Outlook in the Orient." U.S. Naval Institute *Proceedings* 64, no. 6 (June 1938).

"Documents on Naval War with France." U.S. Naval Institute *Proceedings* 61, no. 4 (April 1935).

The Eclipse of American Sea Power. New York: American Army and Navy Journal, 1922.

"The Elements of Leadership." U.S. Naval Institute *Proceedings* 46, no. 12 (December 1920).

"A Forgotten Fight in Florida." U.S. Naval Institute *Proceedings* 62, no. 4 (April 1936).

"The Founders of the American Navy." *Records of the American Catholic Historical Society of Philadelphia,* Spring 1946.

"The General Problem of Naval Warfare." U.S. Naval Institute *Proceedings* 42, no. 1 (January–February 1916).

"The Great Lesson from Nelson for Today." U.S. Naval Institute *Proceedings* 40, no. 2 (March–April 1914).

A History of the United States Navy. New York: Putnam's Sons, 1936.

"On the Importance of Leadership." U.S. Naval Institute *Proceedings* 46, no. 3 (March 1920).

"The Japanese Situation." U.S. Naval Institute *Proceedings* 61, no. 9 (September 1935).

"Japan's Drive for World Trade." U.S. Naval Institute *Proceedings* 60, no. 10 (October 1934).

"The London Treaty and American Naval Policy." U.S. Naval Institute *Proceedings* 57, no. 8 (August 1931).

"The Nation Notes and Long Remembers . . . : Seapower's Decisive Influence in the Civil War, Part I." *Navy* 4, no. 1 (January 1961). (With Ernest M. Eller)

"The Nation Notes and Long Remembers . . . : Seapower's Decisive Influence in the Civil War, Part II." *Navy* 4, no. 2 (February 1961). (With Ernest M. Eller)

"Naval Campaigns of the Future." *Marine Corps Gazette* 34, no. 7 (July 1950).

Naval Documents Related to the Quasi-War between the United States and France, vols. 1–7. Washington, D.C.: Navy Department, 1935–37. (Editor)

The Naval Genius of George Washington. Boston: Houghton Mifflin, 1932.

"The Naval Historical Foundation." U.S. Naval Institute *Proceedings* 73, no. 12 (December 1947).

"Naval Personnel Legislation." U.S. Naval Institute *Proceedings* 39, no. 4 (December 1913).

"Naval Power as a Preserver of Neutrality and Peace." U.S. Naval Institute *Proceedings* 63, no. 5 (May 1937).

"Naval Reduction and Parity." *Scientific American,* October 1929.

"Naval Shelling of the Federal Council." *Literary Digest,* July 1929.

Naval Sketches of the War in California—Reproducing Twenty-Eight Drawings Made in 1846–47, by William H. Meyers, Gunner on the U.S. Sloop-of-War Dale—Descriptive Text by Capt. Dudley W. Knox, USN. Introduction by Franklin D. Roosevelt. New York: Random House, 1939. (Editor)

"The Navy and the National Life." U.S. Naval Institute *Proceedings* 60, no. 6 (June 1934).

"The Navy and Public Indoctrination." U.S. Naval Institute *Proceedings* 55, no. 6 (June 1929).

"A New Source of American Naval History." U.S. Naval Institute *Proceedings* 56, no. 7 (July 1930).

"An Object Lesson for America." *Argonaut* 117, no. 3176 (September 1938).

"Old Principles and Modern Applications." U.S. Naval Institute *Proceedings* 40, no. 4 (July–August 1914).

"One Year after the Naval Conference." *Outlook,* December 1922.

"Our Post-War Mission." U.S. Naval Institute *Proceedings* 45, no. 8 (August 1919).

"Our Stake in Sea Power." U.S. Naval Institute *Proceedings* 53, no. 10 (October 1927).

"Our Vanishing History and Traditions." U.S. Naval Institute *Proceedings* 52, no. 1 (January 1926).

"Peace and the Navy." *Atlantic Monthly,* April 1938.

"Porter's Dire Need of Bases." U.S. Naval Institute *Proceedings* 59, no. 11 (November 1933).

"Recent Developments in Limitation of Naval Armaments." U.S. Naval Institute *Proceedings* 52, no. 10 (October 1926).

"The Role of Doctrine in Naval Warfare." U.S. Naval Institute *Proceedings* 41, no. 2 (March–April 1915).

"Sea Power and Pocketbooks." U.S. Naval Institute *Proceedings* 51, no. 12 (December 1925).

"Sea Power. What Is It?" *Marine Corps Gazette* 20, no. 4 (November 1936).

"Ships, from Dugouts to Dreadnoughts." *National Geographic* 73 (January 1938).

"The Ships that Count." U.S. Naval Institute *Proceedings* 59, no. 7 (July 1933).

"Should the London Treaty Be Ratified?" *Congressional Digest*, June 1930.

"Some Naval Aspects of the War Debt Question." U.S. Naval Institute *Proceedings* 58, no. 5 (May 1932).

"Some Underlying Principles of Morale." U.S. Naval Institute *Proceedings* 42, no. 6 (November–December 1916).

"Trade." U.S. Naval Institute *Proceedings* 53, no. 11 (November 1927).

"Trained Initiative and Unity of Action: The True Bases of Military Efficiency." U.S. Naval Institute *Proceedings* 39, no. 1 (March 1913).

"The United States Navy Between the World Wars." In *History of United States Naval Operations in World War II: The Battle of the Atlantic, 1939–1943*, by Samuel Eliot Morison. Boston: Little Brown, 1947.

"Washington Views Naval Preparedness." U.S. Naval Institute *Proceedings* 58, no. 8 (August 1932).

ABOUT THE EDITOR

David Kohnen earned a PhD with the Laughton Chair of Naval History at the University of London (King's College London). He is the author of *Commanders Winn and Knowles: Winning the U-Boat War with Intelligence,* among several other scholarly works. On active and reserve status in the U.S. Navy, he completed two deployments afloat in Middle Eastern waters, two ashore in Iraq, and one supporting operations in Afghanistan. Kohnen serves on the faculty at the National Intelligence University in Washington, D.C. He also teaches in the Maritime History Department and College of Operations and Strategic Leadership at the Naval War College. He lives in Rhode Island with his wife, Sarah, and daughters, Elisabeth and Katherine.

The Naval Institute Press is the book-publishing arm of the U.S. Naval Institute, a private, nonprofit, membership society for sea service professionals and others who share an interest in naval and maritime affairs. Established in 1873 at the U.S. Naval Academy in Annapolis, Maryland, where its offices remain today, the Naval Institute has members worldwide.

Members of the Naval Institute support the education programs of the society and receive the influential monthly magazine *Proceedings* or the colorful bimonthly magazine *Naval History* and discounts on fine nautical prints and on ship and aircraft photos. They also have access to the transcripts of the Institute's Oral History Program and get discounted admission to any of the Institute-sponsored seminars offered around the country.

The Naval Institute's book-publishing program, begun in 1898 with basic guides to naval practices, has broadened its scope to include books of more general interest. Now the Naval Institute Press publishes about seventy titles each year, ranging from how-to books on boating and navigation to battle histories, biographies, ship and aircraft guides, and novels. Institute members receive significant discounts on the Press' more than eight hundred books in print.

Full-time students are eligible for special half-price membership rates. Life memberships are also available.

For a free catalog describing Naval Institute Press books currently available, and for further information about joining the U.S. Naval Institute, please write to:

Member Services
U.S. Naval Institute
291 Wood Road
Annapolis, MD 21402-5034
Telephone: (800) 233-8764
Fax: (410) 571-1703
Web address: www.usni.org